I KNOW
ABSOLUTELY
NOTHING
A B O U T ™
GOLF

I KNOW
ABSOLUTELY
NOTHING
A B O U T™
GOLF

A New Golfer's Guide to
the Game's Traditions, Rules,
Etiquette, Equipment, and
Language

Steve Eubanks and Whitney Crouse

Rutledge Hill Press
Nashville, Tennessee

Published in Nashville, Tennessee, by Rutledge Hill Press, 211 Seventh Avenue North, Nashville, Tennessee 37219.

Distributed in Canada by H. B. Fenn & Company, Ltd., 34 Nixon Road, Bolton, Ontario, Canada L7E 1W2.

Distributed in Australia by Millennium Books, 33 Maddox Street, Alexandria NSW 2015.

Distributed in New Zealand by Tandem Press, 2 Rugby Road, Birkenhead, Auckland 10.

Distributed in the United Kingdom by Verulam Publishing, Ltd., 152a Park Street Lane, Park Street, St. Albans, Hertfordshire AL2 2AU.

Design by Harriette Bateman

Typography by D&T Bailey Typesetting, Inc., Nashville, Tennessee

Inside illustrations by David Alden

Library of Congress Cataloging-in-Publication Data

Eubanks, Steve, 1962–
    I know absolutely nothing about golf / Steve Eubanks and Whitney Crouse.
       p.   cm.
    ISBN: 1-55853-342-7
    1. Golf.   I. Crouse, Whitney, 1958–   .   II. Title.
GV965.C76   1996
796.352—dc20   96-18151
                                                                   CIP

Printed in the United States of America

    2   3   4   5   6   7   8   9—99   98   97   96

CONTENTS

	Acknowledgments	vii
	Introduction	ix
1.	The Challenge	1
2.	This Silly Game Explained	7
3.	The Course, of Course	21
4.	Getting Clubbed	35
5.	A Lesson on Lessons	51
6.	Everything but the Kitchen Sink	59
7.	Where to Tee It Up	71
8.	The Great Equalizer	79
9.	The Rules of the Road	89
10.	Behave Yourself	99
11.	Meeting the Challenge	109
12.	Elmer's Glossary	113

ACKNOWLEDGMENTS

When we first began this project we could have qualified as the lead characters in another book with the title *I Know Absolutely Nothing about Publishing a Book*. Fortunately, we had plenty of help along the way. Those who deserve immeasurable credit include our illustrator, David Alden, whose talent and wit never cease to amaze us; our editor, Mike Towle, who walked us through the publishing maze with avuncular patience; our publisher, Larry Stone; and most importantly, our wives, Lisa Crouse and Debbie Eubanks, without whom nothing is possible.

INTRODUCTION

In the last century, more has been written about the game of golf than all other amateur and professional sports combined. Thousands of books and periodicals on golf are in circulation, with more being printed every day. Golf is the most technically analyzed sport in athletic history. Tens of thousands of experts deliver hundreds of thousands of instructional tips, theories, and historical perspectives on the game. Entire publishing houses, video production companies, and public relations firms have been built around golf, golf instruction, and the basic tenet that people want to read, learn, and know all there is to know about this game.

Why did we think you needed another golf book? Simple. Two million people a year are taking up the game. That's almost fifty-five hundred people a day entering this foreign, almost cultlike culture we call golf. And, surprisingly, no one has ever provided a tool for those who can honestly say, "I know absolutely nothing about golf."

This book is for those two million newcomers to golf a year, along with all the rest of you who are tired of listening in abject ignorance while the weekend golf match gets rehashed in strange jargon over Monday morning coffee. If you're sick of being relegated to an outlet mall because you didn't sign up for the business-trip golf outing, this is for you.

A word of warning: If your only golfing objective at this point is to lower your handicap from thirty to eighteen, you need to close the cover and move on. But if you think a golf handicap is something covered under the Americans with Disabilities Act, then you've picked up the right book. Similarly, if you mistake a one-iron for a high-grade cooking utensil, or you guess that Balata is a southern Ukrainian province, you are in the right place. This is your guide to a unique world in which rub of the green has nothing to do with color and fore-play is something you want to avoid. *I Know Absolutely Nothing about™ Golf* is your introduction to the sometimes quirky, occasionally funny, oftentimes frustrating and confusing—but always special—game millions love and cherish.

Having grown up around golf and having taught hundreds of people how to play, we recognize that the number-one obstacle for new golfers is anxiety. People feel they should know more than they do. Nobody wants to admit total ignorance, and no one wants to be embarrassed by saying or doing the wrong things when they are just starting out. On the other hand, no one likes being condescended to either. That's why we wrote this book. There are no cute rhymes, no corny sayings (we hope), and nothing that insults your basic intellect. Anxiety about knowing absolutely nothing about golf is not a crime. We promise not to treat you like a criminal or a moron.

Even though you'll find that golfers are some of the most engaging people you'll ever meet, chances are better than average that you won't receive the kind of "spend the day with us" service our main character finds on her first day of learning golf. That's another reason we wrote the book. Golfers typically are friendly, patient, and kind, but climbing the learning curve can be trying, not just on you, but also on those who are teaching you. This book takes those worries away.

Whether you are planning to play golf for the first time or you just want to discover what makes chasing a little white ball so infectious, we believe you've picked the perfect starting point. So turn the page and begin a wonderful journey into the ever-growing, ever-changing game of a lifetime.

Welcome to golf.

I KNOW
ABSOLUTELY
NOTHING
A B O U T ™
GOLF

ONE

THE CHALLENGE

Kathleen, who knows absolutely nothing about golf, straightens her scarf as she opens the door to her twenty-fifth-floor office.

She glances at the sign with her name on it as she thinks about the weekly tasks ahead. As founder and president of a successful advertising agency, Kathleen thrives on the rigors of a small business, never shrinking from a challenge such as new business development. She thinks about the potential clients she needs to contact as she walks down the hall, past the walnut-paneled conference room, and into the kitchen for her first cup of strong black coffee.

"Morning, boss," says Jim, a senior account executive. He's holding a cup and talking to Mark, the agency's creative director.

"Hi, guys," she says, reaching into the cabinet for a clean mug. The men continue their discussion.

"Anyway, I'm 160 from the pin and he's IN JAIL

on the right. Now mind you, I've been STAKING IT all day, only to have him DRAIN every SNAKE he looks at. We're all even with one to play."

Kathleen doesn't look up. *Drains every snake? Staking it? What are they talking about?*

"The guy's at least 190 so deep in the GORSE he can't see his feet. The next thing I know, he PUNCHES it out QUAIL HIGH. It rolls a mile, trickles through the FROG HAIR, and stops right on the dance floor."

This is the strangest conversation Kathleen has ever heard. She takes more time than normal to find the right mug. Maybe if she listens a little longer, she'll figure this out.

"What happened?" Mark asks.

"I raked a NICKEL, actually caught a FLYER, and you're not going to believe what happened."

Of course not! Tell us.

"What?"

"It hit the PIN, WRAPPED UP IN THE FLAG, and dropped next to the cup for a GIMME."

Both men laugh.

"You won the hole?" Mark asks.

"He LIPPED out for the HALVE. I won, one-up."

By now Kathleen has poured her coffee and run out of excuses to remain in the kitchen. "What are you two talking about?" she finally inquires.

"Oh, nothing," Mark answers. "Just golf. Jim had a big match this weekend."

"Oh."

Kathleen smiles and excuses herself. *Golf.* Of all the things it could have been, golf never entered her mind. She's never played golf, although many clients invite her to play, and she's embarrassed to admit she knows nothing about the game.

In her office, Kathleen settles behind her desk and starts to plan the week. There's copy to approve, bluelines to review, and most importantly, potential clients to call. She's examining a short list of prospects when her secretary buzzes.

"Kathleen, Mr. Davis is on line one."

She quickly picks up the phone. C. P. Davis is her oldest client and a revered mentor.

"C. P., how's that new ad doing?"

"Great. We've had all sorts of comments on it. I think this one's a real winner."

"Thanks. It's always comforting to hear good news."

"It's comforting to be able to give it," he comments. "But look, I'm calling about more important things than work."

What could possibly be more important than work to C. P. Davis?

"I'm putting together a golf outing for my best friends and clients. I'd like you to play."

"Golf?" she echoes.

"Yes, golf. You know, clubs, balls, fore—all that good stuff."

She doesn't know, and she swallows hard before responding.

"C. P., I know absolutely nothing about golf."

"It's time you learned. I want my friends to meet the marketing wizard who creates my ads."

"I . . . uh . . . "

"No buts, Kathleen. I've generated more new business on the golf course than I can count, and there's no better place than on a golf course to meet new people or to entertain clients. It's time you learned to play."

"It is?"

"I'm putting an invitation in the mail today. It's a scramble, so you don't have to worry about making a fool of yourself."

The message is loud and clear, except the *scramble* part. "I'll be there," Kathleen replies.

"Great! And don't worry about a thing. You've got a whole month to learn a game I've tried to master for forty years." C. P. laughs and hangs up.

Now you've done it. How are you going to learn everything there is to know about golf in a month?

She sits straight up in her chair and does what she always does in situations like this—she goes to work. To her surprise the Yellow Pages actually has a listing for golf courses.

As someone who makes her living being creative, Kathleen is amazed by the names people choose for golf courses: Raccoon Run, Fox Creek, Possum Lake, Oak Hills, Pine Forest, and Quail Hollow, to name a few. She decides to add golf courses to the list of prospective businesses that could use her help.

By the time she reaches the *S's,* she's convinced all courses look the same in print, so she stops at Shady Oaks. *Just pick up the phone and you're on your way. It's just a game. How tough can it be?* She dials the number.

"Good morning, Shady Oaks, Robert Jones speaking," an elderly gentleman answers.

"Hi, Mr. Jones, I hope you can help me. I know absolutely nothing about golf, which wouldn't be a problem, but, you see, I have to play in an outing next month—"

"Oh my, you do have a problem," Mr. Jones commiserates.

"Yes, well, can anyone at Shady Oaks help me?"

"You've called the right place, and I might say, you're lucky I answered the phone."

Kathleen smiles. "Why's that, Mr. Jones?"

"I'm the locker room attendant here…have been for more than fifty years. I've seen this game go from hickory shafts to boron-graphite. You know, I've had the likes of Ben Hogan, Sam Snead, Arnold Palmer, and Jack Nicklaus right here in this clubhouse, so I don't think anybody can tell you more about the game than I can."

She smiles again and silently agrees with Mr. Jones's assessment: She *is* lucky he answered the phone. "Great. When can we meet?"

"Why don't you come out to Shady Oaks tomorrow morning? Is nine o'clock good for you?"

She checks her schedule. "Nine is great, and I'm sorry I haven't introduced myself. My name's Kathleen."

"Fine, Kathleen. Meet me for a cup of coffee here in the clubhouse. I'll see to it you don't leave without knowing all you need to know about this lovely game."

"Thanks, Mr. Jones. I'll see you tomorrow morning." Kathleen hangs up and runs her hands through her hair. *What have I gotten myself into?*

Two

This Silly Game Explained

Kathleen sits in the grillroom at Shady Oaks Golf Club, sipping coffee and feeling relaxed. Finding the club and getting comfortable in the beautiful Tudor clubhouse was easy. Liking Mr. Robert Jones is even easier. He's tall and handsome, with a full head of wavy, gray hair. His chiseled face is locked in a perpetual smile, which matches his demeanor. Kathleen notices his hands are covered with shoe polish as he sits to talk to her.

"So, Mr. Jones, tell me about the game of golf."

"It's a wonderful old game, Kathleen, rich with tradition. But I'm getting ahead of myself already." He sips his coffee and sits up a little straighter. "The object of golf is to hit a small, white ball as few times as possible into a hole that could be anywhere from one hundred to six hundred yards away. Sounds simple, doesn't it?"

"Not really."

"Oh, sure it is." He laughs. "Each person must hit his or her ball the desired distance and direction using a variety of clubs that come in an assortment of lengths, LOFTS, and shapes."

Kathleen begins taking notes, and Mr. Jones laughs at his new pupil's enthusiasm. "I'd better stick to the basics. We've got plenty of people around the club who can help you with the details."

She looks up and returns his infectious smile.

"You know, Winston Churchill once said, 'Golf is a game whose aim is to hit a very small ball into an even smaller hole, with weapons singularly ill-designed for that purpose.'"

"How can you get the ball into the hole if the hole is smaller than the ball?" she inquires.

Mr. Jones laughs. "Oh, it's not really smaller. That was just Churchill's way of saying it's a difficult game, one that has frustrated golfers for hundreds of years.

"But anyway, each attempt to hit the ball is called a STROKE. Your score on a particular hole is the number of strokes it takes to get the ball into the hole, and your total score for the round is the sum of all your strokes for eighteen holes. The lower your score, the better you've done. That's golf."

"Doesn't sound very interesting," Kathleen observes.

"Oh, you really don't know anything about golf, do you?"

"Absolutely nothing. I can't understand people's fascination. I mean, some of the staff in my office seem obsessed by it."

"Once you've played, you'll know why. Golf has

been stirring romantic emotions in people for years. It doesn't matter if you're a president, a prince, or somebody like me who shines shoes for a living. This game will enchant you, humble you, inspire you, and leave you cursing a blue streak."

Kathleen leans forward on one elbow. "Tell me, what's so fascinating about this game?"

Mr. Jones sips his coffee and ponders the question. "I suspect it's partly due to the fact that golf is played outside in the sunshine and fresh air. Maybe it's because no two golf holes or golf courses are alike."

She shakes her head. "You can say that about a lot of other activities. There has to be more to it."

Mr. Jones rubs his chin and examines the design of the ceiling. "I never thought about that, but you're right. Maybe it's because you can play golf all your life, or maybe it's because no matter how good you are, you'll never master it completely. Whether you play by yourself or with your friends, it's just you against the golf course and you against yourself."

She nods. "It's sort of like skiing or mountain climbing."

"Sort of, yes."

Kathleen returns to her notepad. "You said there are eighteen holes. Why eighteen?"

"I'm glad you asked. Golf has its fair share of folklore, and it was in Scotland that many of golf's fables began. The legend behind the origin of eighteen holes is one of those. As the story goes, the first golf courses were designed on a daily basis by the KEEPER

OF THE GREENS. He would simply go out and cut holes as he saw fit. One day there might be twelve holes, the next day there might be twenty-two. However, each of the Scotsmen who played carried a leather flask of single-malt whiskey, to keep warm in the cold Scottish wind, you know. Each flask held eighteen shots of whiskey, and since no able-bodied Scot would stay out on the course without his drink, there are now eighteen holes on a golf course."

"That's an incredible story," Kathleen says.

"Oh, that's nothing. Golf history is full of incredible stories."

"Who invented the game, the Scots?"

"That's the subject of considerable debate."

Mr. Jones relays several theories on the origins of golf, some dating back to the days of the Roman empire. The Dutch also played a similar game called KOLVEN, he says, in which they used a club and a ball and often played on ice. Another theory says that the Belgian game CHOLE is where golf originated, but, as Mr. Jones quickly points out, nobody really knows for sure.

The most romantic theory is that golf was invented by a shepherd tending his flock in St. Andrews, Scotland. Quite by accident, the shepherd struck a pebble with his crook and the pebble flew straight into a rabbit's hole. When the shepherd was challenged by a companion to do it again, the game of golf was born. Whether fact or fiction, the Royal and Ancient Golf Club at St. Andrews is recognized as the world's oldest golf course.

Mr. Jones takes great pride in his storytelling, and Kathleen is a willing listener. When all the folklore is put aside, he tells her, what can be said for sure is that golf has been played at least five hundred years. The first official record goes back to 1457, the year in which the Scottish King James II had Parliament outlaw golf because his men's preoccupation with the game kept them from practicing archery.

"So you see," Mr. Jones says with a wry grin, "even that long ago golf was a passion greater than national defense."

Kathleen smiles and nods in agreement. "I guess the game migrated to America with the British," she reflects.

Mr. Jones concurs. In the mid-1800s the game was firmly established in England and Scotland, and in 1888 golf crossed the Atlantic when three Scotsmen built the first golf club in the United States in Yonkers, New York. Appropriately, they named it St. Andrews.

"That's fascinating," Kathleen declares. "But what about the game today?"

"It's healthier than ever. There are twenty-five million golfers in America playing on more than fifteen thousand golf courses, and you can probably at least double those numbers in terms of worldwide golf. Most golfers still are men, but more than a third of the new players entering the game today are women."

This pleases Kathleen since she's about to join

...AND GOLF WAS BORN...

GOLF HAS BEEN PLAYED FOR
MORE THAN FIVE HUNDRED
YEARS, BUT FIRST CAME TO
THE UNITED STATES IN 1888.

TODAY THERE ARE MORE THAN
25 MILLION GOLFERS AND 15,000
GOLF COURSES IN THE UNITED
STATES. AND MANY MORE
THROUGHOUT THE WORLD.

those ranks. "Is there someone like a commissioner of golf, or a congress, or a league of some kind?"

"There are associations and organizations everywhere golf is played. We have lots of committees at this club that conduct tournaments, oversee the golf course, and generally manage things. But from a worldwide perspective, the two organizations that govern the game are the United States Golf Association, or USGA, headquartered in New Jersey, and the R&A, or Royal and Ancient Golf Club—"

"Let me guess, located in St. Andrews, Scotland?"

"Yes, ma'am. Both groups are separate entities, but they work together to formulate the official rules of golf and maintain the integrity of the game. They also host some of the world's most important golf tournaments."

"These tournaments, are they what I see on television on weekend afternoons?" she asks.

Mr. Jones shakes his head. "Probably not. The PGA, or Professional Golfers' Association of America, is the ruling body of professional golf. The PGA TOUR, which has ties to the PGA, manages the tournaments you see almost every week on television. Other countries and continents have their own tours as well, such as the European Tour and the Asian Tour, making competitive golf truly a worldwide phenomenon.

"In the United States the PGA governs the twenty-three thousand club professionals around the country, which includes the head professional and apprentices at this club. But all golfers, pro or amateur, play by the same rules."

"You mean the USGA and R&A rules, right?" she pursues, just to make sure.

"That's correct."

Kathleen goes back to her notes. "Those important tournaments you mentioned—I see golf on television every week. What are the important tournaments?"

Mr. Jones smiles again and takes another sip of coffee. "Golf has many, many tournaments played at all levels. But golfers from all over the world would agree that the four most important golf events are called the MAJOR CHAMPIONSHIPS."

As Kathleen writes, Mr. Jones proceeds to explain the four majors.

The first major championship of the year is the MASTERS, which is played in early April at the Augusta National Golf Club in Augusta, Georgia. Many people are familiar with the Masters because it unofficially launches the golf season in many areas of the country. People know that when it's Masters week, it's time to dust off the clubs and start thinking about golf again. The other three major championships are the U.S. Open, the British Open, and the PGA Championship. Each of these three is played at a different course each year. If a golfer wins all four of the major tournaments in the same year, he has won what's called the Grand Slam. Nobody's ever done that in the modern era, although one man won an earlier version of the grand slam back in 1930.

THE MEN'S TOUR
MAJOR GOLF
TOURNAMENTS
IN THE WORLD

MASTERS
U.S. OPEN
BRITISH OPEN
PGA
CHAMPIONSHIP

THE PGA
GOVERNS MORE
THAN
TWENTY-THREE
THOUSAND MEN AND
WOMEN CLUB
PROFESSIONALS.
THE PGA TOUR
CONDUCTS THE
TOURNAMENTS YOU
SEE ON TV

"And who was that?" Kathleen asks.

"Bobby Jones, the greatest amateur golfer who ever lived," Mr. Jones says. "Before he was thirty years old, Jones had won the U.S. Open, the U.S. Amateur, the British Open, and the British Amateur, all in the same year; and then he retired from competitive golf to write, practice law, and play exhibitions. He founded the Augusta National Golf Club in 1932 and started the Masters in 1934. He was the most beloved golfer of his time, and an argument could be made that he was the golfer of the century in America."

Kathleen is silent during what is obviously a reverent moment for her elderly teacher. After a quiet pause Mr. Jones continues, "Of course there are many other heroes in golf. Jack Nicklaus and Arnold Palmer are probably the most well known. Jack's won twenty major championships and Arnie eight. Nicklaus is probably recognized as the best golfer ever to play the game, and Arnie, well, Arnie is loved by fans all over the world. He's the game's most charismatic ambassador, and he's probably done more for the growth of golf than any one person in history."

Kathleen stops taking notes and listens intently. "Who are some other famous golfers?" she asks.

"Walter Hagen, a true showman, glamorized golf in the 1920s. In 1945 Byron Nelson won eleven PGA Tour events in a row. That's a record that will probably stand forever. In the 1950s Ben Hogan and Sam Snead were golf's heroes. Hogan is regarded as the best striker of the golf ball ever, and Snead is the winner of more American tournaments than any other man in professional golf . . . eighty-one in all.

"They played here once . . . Hogan and Snead, I mean," he says as he leans forward. "It was in the late 1940s, just after the war, and the club sponsored a match between the great Ben Hogan and Sam Snead. But they didn't get beyond the second hole. Snead wanted a ruling on a DROP. That's where a golfer can pick up his ball and drop it somewhere else because of a special situation. In this case, Snead's ball was in the right rough against a sprinkler box. Understand, this was in the days when sprinklers were new to golf courses. Snead asked Hogan if he knew what the rule was. Hogan, always the diplomat, said, 'I don't know, Sam. I've never seen one of those in the middle of the fairway.'

"Golf's great international flavor and heritage is evident in the abundance of legendary golfers worldwide, such as South Africa's Gary Player and Bobby Locke; Japan's Jumbo Ozaki and Isao Aoki; England's Harry Vardon and Henry Cotton; Scotland's James Braid; Argentina's Roberto DeVicenzo; New Zealand's Bob Charles; and Australia's Peter Thomson. In fact, Vardon won the British Open a record six times."

"Are there any famous women golfers?" Kathleen inquires.

"Absolutely. How poor of me to forget. Babe Zaharias for one. She won five gold medals in track and field in the 1932 Olympics, then turned her attention to golf and went on to win ten major women's golf championships. Babe also was one of the founding members of the LADIES PROFESSIONAL GOLF ASSOCIATION, or LPGA. That's the women's equivalent to the PGA Tour."

"Quite an athlete," Kathleen observes.

"Yes, ma'am. Of course there's also Mickey Wright, winner of thirteen major tournaments and eighty-two professional wins in all. And Kathy Whitworth, who's won eighty-eight LPGA events. Just like their male counterparts, women also have four major championships that comprise a grand-slam opportunity—the Dinah Shore Classic, the LPGA Championship, the du Maurier Classic, and the U.S. Women's Open."

Mr. Jones pauses and Kathleen notices a twinkle in his eye as he gets lost in his thoughts. "They've all been here. I even shined—"

She stops him before he can get too sentimental. "I'm honored you introduced me to golf, Mr. Jones. This is a great start."

"If you're going to play in a tournament so soon, you'd better learn a little about the golf course and how the game is played. Let me have one of our CADDIES drive you out to see our golf course SUPERINTENDENT, Mr. Murray."

With that, Kathleen and Mr. Jones head outside.

GREAT MEN GOLFERS

BOBBY JONES —THE GREATEST AMATEUR GOLFER

JACK NICKLAUS —THE GREATEST GOLFER EVER, WITH 20 MAJOR TITLES

ARNOLD PALMER—THE MOST CHARISMATIC GOLFER

BEN HOGAN —THE BEST STRIKER OF A GOLF BALL

BYRON NELSON —WON 11 TOURNAMENTS IN ROW

HARRY VARDON —WON BRITISH OPEN SIX TIMES

GREAT WOMEN GOLFERS OF ALL TIME

BABE ZAHARIAS —OLYMPIC TRACK STAR WHO WON 10 MAJOR TOURNAMENTS AND FOUNDED THE LPGA

MICKEY WRIGHT—WON 13 MAJORS AND HAD 82 WINS IN ALL

KATHY WHITWORTH—WON 88 LPGA EVENTS IN HER CAREER

THREE

THE COURSE, OF COURSE

The trip to William Murray's office at the golf course maintenance building is an adventurous one. At Mr. Jones's request, Tony the Caddy fetches a golf cart, picks up Kathleen, and takes off with all the gusto of a Grand Prix driver. Not one to criticize, Kathleen finds herself putting a white-knuckle death grip on the nearest handle as Tony speeds along the path. They pass a beautifully manicured patch of short grass that Kathleen correctly assumes is a GREEN. Then they cross what she presumes to be a FAIRWAY. Just when Kathleen starts to relax her grip, Tony whips the cart into a hairpin turn, bounces through a stand of pine trees, and rattles to a halt in front of a long metal building.

The gravel parking area is littered with equipment ranging from what Kathleen recognizes as a tractor to huge mowers with spiderlike arms carrying bladed reels.

"Mr. Murray is in his office," Tony notes.

Kathleen thanks him and walks into the building. It's a well-lit area similar to the garage where Kathleen gets her car serviced. There are signs on the wall promoting worker safety and a bulletin board with a daily schedule posted. The facility smells of a strange mixture of grass and diesel fuel.

Kathleen walks toward the office in the corner, noticing another sign: William Murray, Superintendent. She knocks.

"It's open."

She opens the door tentatively. William Murray is sitting at his desk working on a laptop computer and is surrounded by volumes of technical books on agronomy, entomology, and chemistry. A walkie-talkie sits on his desk.

Kathleen begins to relax a little. This man is a scientist. She can learn a lot here.

"You must be Kathleen," he greets her, extending his hand. "Robert called down and said you were coming."

"Yes, Mr. Murray."

"Please, call me Will. My father is Mr. Murray."

"Will, I appreciate your seeing me so soon."

"So, you want to know about my golf course," Will comments with a large smile.

"That's right. You see, I know absolutely nothing about golf and—"

"You have one month to learn. I heard." Will sits back at his desk and props his feet up.

"Let's start with the basics," Will declares. "There are more than fifteen thousand golf courses in the

United States and many thousands of others else-where in the world, and no two are exactly alike. Some are flat. Some are hilly. Some have lots of ponds and lakes; some have few or none. That's what makes it so much fun to play a new golf course.

"Most courses have eighteen holes, and a complete round of golf is considered to be eighteen holes. But some courses have only nine holes: you play those twice to arrive at an eighteen-hole score. Other courses, such as resorts or large country clubs, have twenty-seven, thirty-six, or even seventy-two holes. But eighteen holes is standard in most places. On an eighteen-hole course, the first nine holes are called the FRONT NINE, the second the BACK NINE. When you have completed nine holes and head for the tenth tee you are making the TURN."

Kathleen scribbles down everything. "What about PAR?" she asks. "I've heard of it, but what exactly is it?"

Will puts his feet down and leans forward. "Par is a term referring to the standard of play on a hole or what's expected of a first-class golfer. There are par-three, par-four, and par-five golf holes. That simply refers to the number of strokes a good golfer should take to get from the TEE into the hole."

"Sort of like the way the term is used outside of golf," Kathleen reflects. "The par value of a bond, or subpar effort."

"That's right. On a par-three, a good player will usually make a score of three. On a par-four, the standard is four shots, and so on. The total par for a course is the sum of the pars on each hole. A par of 72 is standard for eighteen-hole courses, but par-70, -71, and even -73 courses are not uncommon.

"There are also what are known as EXECUTIVE GOLF COURSES where the course owner has very little land. Par for these courses ranges from 54 to the high 60s, but these types of courses are uncommon."

Kathleen writes this down. "I'm obviously a beginner, and I won't make a par for a while. What do you call what I will score?"

"A bunch," Will laughs. "No, actually you'll make lots of BOGIES and DOUBLE BOGIES. A bogey is one over par on a hole. So if you score a five on a par-four, you've made bogey. A double bogey is two over par on a hole. A triple bogey is three over par, and so on. If you're really good, you'll have a few BIRDIES. A birdie is one under par on a hole. If par on a hole is five, and you make four—"

"I will have made a birdie," Kathleen interjects as she writes feverishly.

"That's right. Should you ever score two under par on a hole, you will have made an EAGLE."

"Eagle. That makes sense," she observes.

"And if you ever score three under par on a hole, like a score of two on a par-five, you will have made a DOUBLE EAGLE."

"I guess those are pretty rare," she says.

"Extremely. I've seen only one, and it was on a short par-five."

DOUBLE
EAGLE—
THREE UNDER PAR
ON A HOLE.

EAGLE—
TWO UNDER PAR
ON A HOLE.

BIRDIE—
ONE UNDER PAR
ON A HOLE.

PAR—
TARGET SCORE ON
A HOLE.

BOGEY—
ONE OVER PAR ON
A HOLE.

DOUBLE
BOGEY—
TWO OVER PAR
ON A HOLE.

"You said short par-five. How long are golf holes, on average?"

"As I said, all golf courses are different, but an average par-three is about 150 yards long for men and 120 yards for women. Some are shorter and some are longer, but that's an average. An average par-four is about 400 yards for men and 300 yards for women. A typical par-five is around 500 yards for men and 400 yards for women. Total yardage for an average eighteen-hole golf course is around 6,500 yards for men and 5,800 yards for women."

Kathleen tries to equate these distances to something she knows. "So, to get a double eagle, you have to hit the ball into the hole on a 500-yard hole in only two shots?"

"Yes, ma'am."

"And that's hard to do?"

Will smiles. "You know much about baseball?"

"A little."

"Then you must know that the center-field wall in most baseball parks is about 400 feet from home plate. That's only about 135 yards. Do you know how hard it is to hit a ball over the center-field fence?"

From her years as an outfielder on a high school softball team, Kathleen knows full well how hard it is. "Yes," she replies.

"Imagine hitting a home run over the center-field wall into the upper deck and intentionally landing it in a beer cup on seat twenty-three, row G. That's sort of what a double eagle is like."

"Oh," she sighs as she writes herself a note not to expect any double eagles in the near future.

"A more common occurrence and perhaps the most exciting moment for a golfer is a HOLE IN ONE. That's when a golfer scores a one, or an eagle, on a par-three. For the average golfer, the odds of a hole in one are one in ten thousand on any given shot for a par-three."

"Have you ever made a hole in one?" Kathleen asks.

"No, but I've seen other folks make them. It's really exciting."

Kathleen makes a mental note this time not to expect any holes in one either. "What other characteristics do all golf courses share?"

"You mean like greens and fairways?"

"Yes, and whatever else."

Will takes a deep breath. "Each hole features

- a teeing ground,
- a fairway,
- ROUGH, usually running along each side of the fairway,
- maybe a few hazards,
- a green,
- and a CUP, or hole."

Kathleen writes. Will continues. "Each hole begins on the tee, or tee box, as it's sometimes called. The tee box is a closely mown area of grass with tee markers on it."

"Tee markers?" she inquires.

"Yes. These are a pair of objects, normally blocks

of wood, stone, or metal, between which you tee up your ball. The rules say you are to tee your ball in an invisible rectangle between those tee markers. In fact, if you tee off in front of the invisible line of the tee markers, it's a penalty."

Kathleen remembers seeing several sets of these markers during her wild ride to the maintenance building. As she recalls, there were more than one pair of markers on each hole. "You have blue, white, and red markers here. I assume that's why the distances you mentioned are different for men and women."

"You're very observant," Will comments. "Golf courses usually have several different tees with corresponding markers. At this club the blue markers are for the better golfers who prefer a longer, tougher golf course. Most male golfers play from the white markers. And the red markers make the course shorter and supposedly easier. Generally, seniors and ladies play from the red markers."

"Chauvinist!" Kathleen exclaims, smiling.

"No, no, don't get me wrong. You can play from any tees you like. Most women prefer the red, or most forward, tees because they don't hit the ball as far as men."

"Sounds like I'll be playing the pink tees." Kathleen and Will both laugh.

She clarifies, "So, the term *tee* describes the area of grass where you start play on a hole?"

"That's right, and it's also the name for the little wooden peg you place your ball on when teeing it up. In fact, you use a tee on a tee box when starting a hole. Got it?"

"Got it," she says, nodding her head.

"The main avenue of play from the tee to the green is called a fairway, although you won't find that word mentioned in the rules of golf."

"Why not?" Kathleen asks.

"I don't know, really. It just shows you how confusing the rules can be. The USGA and the R&A refer to this area of the course as 'through the green' so there's really no distinction in the rules for the fairway. Anyway, the fairway is short grass, usually cut at one-half to three-quarters of an inch in height, and it's the path you want to take when playing a hole."

"Sort of like the yellow brick road," Kathleen says.

"Exactly. Follow the short grass to the hole. If your ball strays outside the fairway, it usually ends up in the rough. Rough grass is normally one to four inches high."

Will gets up and walks over to the chalkboard and draws a golf hole.

"Farther from the yellow brick road, as you say, are HAZARDS. They are ponds, lakes, streams, and ditches, as well as bunkers that can be in the form of either SAND TRAPS or grassy depressions. Sometimes you can play your ball from a hazard, such as when it's in a sand trap. Other times you can't find it at all, such as when it's at the bottom of a pond. On those occasions, you have to add a PENALTY STROKE to your score and hit a new ball."

"Lions and tigers and bears," Kathleen observes.

"Something like that," Will says. "The green is the area of very short grass surrounding the hole where you PUTT the ball."

"Yes, I saw a green on my little joyride out here. It looks like carpet."

"Well, thank you. The greens are mowed as low as an eighth of an inch, and we work like the devil to maintain a smooth, consistent putting surface."

"What's the area of grass I saw surrounding the green? It looked about two feet wide."

"You really are observant. That's the FRINGE, or the COLLAR. It's a buffer between the green and the fairway or rough.

"The green has a cup in it, which, by the way, is only four and a quarter inches in diameter. And as you may already know, the cup has a FLAGSTICK to mark the position of the hole. In fact, we have one DOGLEG here where you can't see the hole—"

"Whoa! A dog-what?"

Will grins. "A dogleg is a hole that curves left or right, like a dog's leg."

"Very clever."

"Yup, those golfers are a clever bunch."

Will sits a little straighter and moves the conversation on to the many different types of grasses that make up a golf course. Kathleen is surprised to learn that many of the hybrid grasses available for lawn use were developed specifically for golf courses. The many strains of BENT GRASS, for example, were developed for putting greens, and the more durable

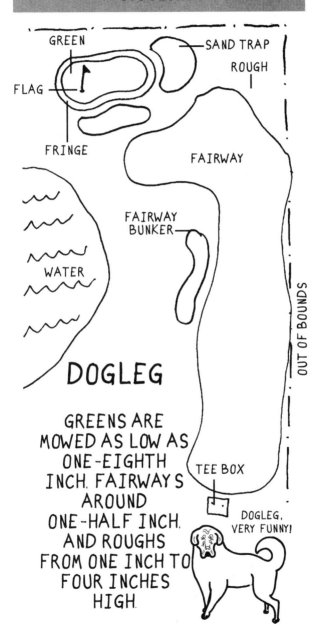

GREEN

FLAG

FRINGE

SAND TRAP

ROUGH

FAIRWAY

FAIRWAY BUNKER

WATER

OUT OF BOUNDS

DOGLEG

GREENS ARE MOWED AS LOW AS ONE-EIGHTH INCH. FAIRWAYS AROUND ONE-HALF INCH. AND ROUGHS FROM ONE INCH TO FOUR INCHES HIGH.

TEE BOX

DOGLEG, VERY FUNNY!

strains of hybrid BERMUDA GRASS were created for use on fairways and roughs. Will is obviously a master at his profession, but his eloquent monologue is taking too long.

She holds up her hand to stop him. "Now remember, I'm not trying to become an agronomist. I'm just trying to prepare for a golf tournament next month."

Will concludes, "Suffice it to say that golf courses have everything from bent and bermuda grasses, to fescues, ryes, buffalo, bahia, zoysia, and everything in between. That's what makes my life interesting."

"And the superintendent is the man in charge of caring for the golf course?" she asks.

"That's me. Years ago we were referred to as the greenkeeper, but today the term *superintendent* is used instead. In fact, the Golf Course Superintendents Association of America, or GCSAA, is the nationwide organization of people such as me."

"Is it expensive to maintain a golf course?" Kathleen's inquiring business mind wants to know.

"It can cost up to a million dollars a year for an eighteen-hole layout, depending on how good you want the course to be. We don't spend that much, but when you talk about labor, chemicals, fertilizer, and irrigation for 175 acres of highly groomed grass, it's expensive."

"Wow," she reacts, dumbfounded. She realizes again how little she really knew. "I guess I now know the basics about the golf course. Anything else I should know at this point?"

"Nope. You've just completed my fabled lecture, Golf Course 101."

"And I'm a proud graduate. Thanks so much for your help."

"Anytime. Now can I have someone drive you back to the clubhouse?"

"On a cart?"

"Yes."

"No thanks. I think I'll walk."

THE SUPERINTENDENT
TAKES CARE OF THE COURSE. HE
USED TO BE CALLED A
GREENKEEPER.

THE ROUGH IS
TOUGH STUFF!

FOUR

GETTING CLUBBED

After a delightful walk across the Shady Oaks golf course, Kathleen arrives back at the clubhouse. In the lobby a helpful member directs her to the pro shop. Within minutes, a handsome young man in his midthirties, wearing slacks and a sports shirt, walks up and extends his hand. "You must be Kathleen. I'm Jack Nickels, the head golf professional."

"Nice to meet you," Kathleen replies.

Jack is trim and polished. Kathleen learns that in addition to being a college graduate in business management, Jack played the American and Asian tours for several years prior to becoming a club professional. As head professional, he gives lessons, conducts tournaments, sells golf equipment, and supervises several assistant golf professionals.

"Robert tells me you're taking a crash course in golf," he says.

"With the exception of what Robert and Will

have taught me so far, I know absolutely nothing about golf. Can you help me?"

"You bet. We love beginners. I assume you don't have any clubs?"

"Not only that, I don't know anything about them," Kathleen answers.

The pro nods. "Okay, then I need to introduce you to our club maker and fitter."

"You have a club maker?"

"Yes, one of the best in the area. He's an assistant professional, but he specializes in golf club fitting and repair. His workshop is downstairs." Jack motions Kathleen to follow and they head down a long, narrow stairwell.

Downstairs, Kathleen enters a brightly lit room filled with workbenches, tools, and metal parts. A young man wearing an apron and safety glasses looks up from a buffing wheel.

"Kathleen, I'd like you to meet Tommy Morris, our resident golf club expert."

The young man puts down his work and enthusiastically shakes Kathleen's hand.

"Tommy, Kathleen needs your help," Jack explains.

"Lots of it," she jumps in. "I know nothing about golf clubs."

"I'd like you to give her an introduction to golf clubs," Jack pursues.

"Sure," Tommy replies.

Jack leaves Kathleen with Tommy. She explains her predicament.

"So, you know nothing about golf clubs?"

"Absolutely nothing."

"Welcome to my basement. I love to talk about golf clubs." Tommy picks up a golf club. "Let's start with the most basic definition. A golf CLUB is any implement used in golf to hit a golf ball. It consists of three components:

- the grip,
- the shaft,
- and the clubhead."

Tommy takes off his safety glasses as Kathleen opens her notepad.

"The GRIP is the part of the club the golfer holds. It's made of either leather or rubber molded into a handle. Grips come in various sizes to fit different-sized hands. While most grips are made of rubber, some golfers like the soft feel of leather, although leather grips are more expensive."

Kathleen draws in her notepad. "What about the other part, the shaft. Is that right?"

"Yes, it is. The SHAFT is just that: a long, thin rod with a grip on one end and a clubhead on the other. Obviously, you hold the club with the grip, and you hit the ball with the clubhead. The shaft connects the two. Now the shaft is important for many reasons. The longer the shaft, the farther you hit the ball."

"Why's that?" Kathleen asks.

"Think about it. The farther out you go on the spoke of a wheel, the faster it goes. The farther out the shaft the clubhead is, the faster it travels."

"So why not make all shafts really long?"

"Good question!" Tommy answers. "Two reasons: You don't want to hit every golf shot a long way; and the longer a club is, the harder it is to control your shot. Try swinging a long broom when you get home, and you'll see what I mean."

"I see."

"Shafts come in a variety of flexes or stiffness. Golfers who swing the club fast need a stiffer shaft than golfers who have a slow, easy swing. There's no universal or official scale of FLEX. Each manufacturer has its own. But in basic terms, shafts come in flexible, or F; regular, denoted by R; stiff, S; and extra stiff—"

"Let me guess, XS?"

"You got it. Regular, or R, shafts are by far the most common, and they fit the majority of golfers. Flex or F shafts are appropriate for a lot of women."

Kathleen looks at the variety of shafts lining one wall of the workshop. "Why are some of them black and others silver?"

"Shafts come in a variety of materials—space-age materials, actually. Sixty years ago they were made of hand-carved hickory. Today most shafts are made of steel, but the black ones you see are graphite. Some are aluminum. There's also titanium, kevlar, and other composite materials. Who knows what'll come next!"

"I guess a lot depends on how well you play and how serious you are about the game," Kathleen observes.

A GOLF CLUB IS ANYTHING USED TO HIT A GOLF BALL. IT CONSISTS OF A GRIP, A SHAFT, AND A — CLUBHEAD. —

A SHEPHERD'S CROOK — THE ORIGINAL WOOD!

— SHAFT —

SHAFTS COME IN VARYING LENGTHS AND FLEXES. THE LONGER THE SHAFT OR CLUB, THE FARTHER YOU HIT THE BALL. SHAFTS WERE ONCE MADE FROM WOOD. TODAY, THEY CAN BE STEEL, TITANIUM, ALUMINUM, OR GRAPHITE.

— GRIP —

"Exactly. The same is true of clubheads. Now pay careful attention because the clubhead has some very important parts. It's the CLUBHEAD that actually hits the ball. The point at which the shaft attaches to the clubhead is called the HOSEL."

"I'm sorry, the what?" Kathleen asks.

"HAH-zul. The hosel. The part of the clubhead that actually hits the ball is the CLUBFACE. The end of the clubhead farthest from the shaft is the TOE, and the closest portion is called the HEEL. The bottom of the clubhead is the SOLE, and the thin lines on the clubface are called GROOVES."

She writes and draws. "What are grooves for?"

"They put spin on the ball."

She's not sure why that's important, but makes a note to ask later.

"You're doing great so far. Let's keep going. Do you see how there are different angles of the clubface in relation to the hosel and shaft?" Tommy holds up two clubs, showing Kathleen the different face angles.

"Yes."

"That's called LOFT. The more loft a club has, the higher the ball will fly. Do you play tennis?"

"I have."

Using tennis as an analogy, Tommy proceeds to explain loft by referring to a tennis racket. To hit a high lob, a tennis player must point the face of the racket angled up at impact, thus giving the return shot more loft. To hit a line drive in tennis, the racket is pointed almost straight away, square to the ball at impact. It's the same in golf. The clubface facing up has a lot of built-in loft and therefore hits the ball high. The clubface that has little angle, or very little loft, hits the ball lower, but conceivably farther.

Tommy then shows Kathleen how golf clubs, both irons and woods, are numbered for identification, with the numbers corresponding to the club's loft. The lower the number, the less loft a club has. The farther a golfer wants to hit a ball, he or she must use a correspondingly lower-numbered club. To better illustrate this principle, Tommy holds up a nine-iron and points to the relatively high loft of the clubface. Kathleen understands the concept and can easily see that a nine-iron is used for hitting high, short shots. On the other hand, a one-iron has very little loft and therefore hits the ball lower and farther.

"Okay, but the nine-iron is also shorter than the one-iron," Kathleen says as she demonstrates, holding the nine-iron in her left hand and the one-iron in her right. "Is that because you want to hit the nine-iron a shorter distance?"

"Precisely. You don't want to hit all your shots the same distance, just as you don't want to hit them all the same height. When you're a short distance from the hole, you want the ball to go shorter and higher and stop on the green. Sort of like pitching horseshoes. You lob the ball high and short with the shorter, higher-numbered clubs.

"Conversely, you hit the ball farther and lower with the longer, less-lofted clubs. When you're a

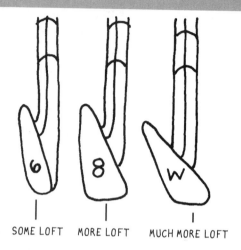

SOME LOFT   MORE LOFT   MUCH MORE LOFT

THE MORE LOFT A CLUB HAS, THE
HIGHER AND SHORTER THE
CLUB WILL HIT A BALL, AND
VICE VERSA. GOLF CLUBS
ARE NUMBERED FOR
IDENTIFICATION— THE LOWER
THE NUMBER, THE LESS LOFT
A CLUB HAS BUT THE FARTHER
IT WILL HIT THE BALL.

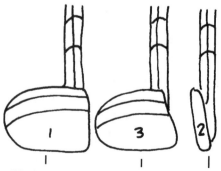

VERY, VERY LITTLE LOFT   VERY LITTLE LOFT   LITTLE LOFT

long way from the hole, that's what you want; but remember, the longer the club is, the harder it is to control."

Kathleen writes this down. But Tommy wants to make sure she has it in her head, not just on paper.

"Okay, let's take a little test," he announces. "What's a five-iron?"

She looks puzzled.

"Think about it," he encourages.

"Okay, it's a medium-length club with medium loft for midrange shots."

"Perfect! See, you know more about golf than you thought."

"I still feel like a dummy."

"Don't. You'll get there. Let's talk about the different types of clubs."

"I thought we just did."

"There's more. The types of clubs I'm talking about now are WOODS, IRONS, and PUTTERS."

"Sounds complicated."

"It's not. Let's start with woods. Woods are the longest clubs in your bag. They also have the least amount of loft, so they're used to hit the ball—"

"Longer distances," she interjects.

"That's right. Most golfers TEE OFF, or begin play on a hole, with a wood in order to hit the longest shot."

She adds this to her notes. "I assume they're made of wood since they're called woods."

"You would think so, wouldn't you? That once was true, but the term *wood* now refers to any club that has the characteristics of an old style wooden club." Tommy points to the clubs on his rack. "Today's woods are made of graphite, metal, or one of many other high-tech composite materials. In fact, the most popular woods in use today are called 'metal woods.' How's that for being confusing?"

"Pretty confusing, but I think I've got it. The name is just a carryover from when all these clubs were made of wood."

"Correct. They are also numbered just like irons. The longest-hitting club in any golf bag is the one-wood, often called a DRIVER. Because it has the least loft and longest length of any golf club, the driver is the hardest club to hit well. As a beginner, you might want to avoid using a driver until you get proficient at the game."

"Which might take a while," she concedes.

"Not really. Learning golf is easier than it used to be because modern equipment is so sophisticated.

"As the loft of a wood increases, so does the identifying number. Woods numbered three or higher are often referred to as FAIRWAY WOODS because they are designed to hit the ball off the ground, not off a tee. It's not uncommon to see woods numbered as high as seven, eight, or nine."

"Will Murray said that a tee is the small wooden peg used to hold the ball up off the ground," Kathleen comments. "It's supposed to make it easier to hit the ball, but you can't use it all the time, right?"

"Right. You may use a tee only when you're beginning play on a hole."

"Okay, back to clubs." Kathleen has her pencil ready.

Tommy reviews the loft and length mechanics of irons, showing Kathleen how each iron has distinct characteristics. He shows her how clubs are numbered one through nine and how the most-lofted irons (which could be considered numbers ten and eleven) are actually called "the pitching wedge" and the SAND WEDGE. After feverishly recording all this information, Kathleen still seems a bit overwhelmed, so Tommy decides to simplify things.

"The most important thing to remember about golf clubs is that there are hundreds of brands and models," he clarifies. "As a beginner, you want the ones that are easiest to hit. PERIMETER-WEIGHTED, or CAVITY-BACKED, clubs are great for beginners."

"Perimeter what?" she asks.

"Perimeter weighted, but don't try to master the technical stuff yet. Just remember that these are the easiest clubs for beginners because the sweet spot is much larger."

"Sweet spot?"

"Yes, the SWEET SPOT is the center portion of the clubface that imparts a terrific feel and makes for a better shot. Perimeter-weighted clubs make it easier to hit the ball well because of a larger sweet spot."

Now that he has explained irons and woods, Tommy turns the discussion to putters, usually the smallest club in the bag, but often the most outrageous in terms of design.

IRONS

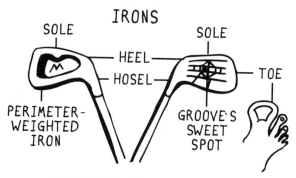

SOLE
HEEL
HOSEL
PERIMETER-WEIGHTED IRON

SOLE
TOE
GROOVE'S SWEET SPOT

CAVITY-BACK, OR PERIMETER-WEIGHTED, IRONS HAVE A LARGER SWEET SPOT AND ARE EASIER TO HIT

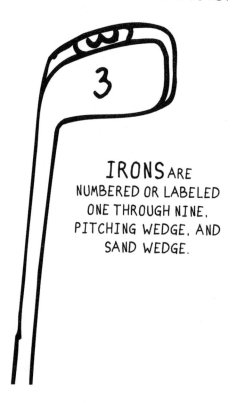

IRONS ARE NUMBERED OR LABELED ONE THROUGH NINE, PITCHING WEDGE, AND SAND WEDGE.

"A putter is the club used to hit, or should I say 'roll,' the ball on the green. Most golfers believe this is the most important club they own. It has almost no loft and it's generally the shortest club."

"I know this one. Anyone who has played miniature golf recognizes a putter. It's the same, right?"

"Right. Except golfers use better putters than the ones at miniature golf courses. You don't have to putt your ball through a dragon's mouth on a real golf course."

They both laugh.

"Before you buy a putter, try a few and choose the one that feels right for you," Tommy says. "It doesn't matter what it looks like as long as it works."

"Counting woods, irons, and putters, how many clubs are in a golf bag?"

"The rules say you're only allowed to carry fourteen."

"The USGA and R&A rules, right?"

Tommy is surprised. "Right. See, you *do* know something about this game."

"More than I ever thought I would," she declares.

"The fourteen clubs can be any combination of woods, irons, or putters, but no more than fourteen are allowed. If this rule didn't exist, golfers would show up to play with a small arsenal of clubs. Obviously, you've never bought clubs. Do you have any idea how expensive they are?"

She braces herself for the worst. "No, how expensive are they?"

"Anywhere from a few hundred dollars to several thousand. As a beginner, you shouldn't buy a premium set. A good starter set might have ten to twelve inexpensive new or used clubs. You should try to get a three- and five-wood, irons numbered four through nine, a pitching wedge, and a putter. Check the newspaper. Lots of people sell old clubs. Plus, there are hundreds of golf discount stores you can check out. Of course, my advice is for you to see a golf professional. A qualified pro can put you in a good first set at a reasonable cost."

Returning, Jack opens the door to the workshop and joins them. "Looks like technology has changed the game of golf quite a bit," Kathleen observes.

"Yes, but not as much as you might think."

She looks puzzled.

"Don't get me wrong, golf equipment has evolved considerably, but clubs look pretty much the same as they did when the game began. That's because the USGA and R&A have strict equipment guidelines."

"Mr. Jones told me those organizations guard the integrity of the game. I guess that's what he meant."

Tommy and Jack both nod.

"Yes, that's part of it," Jack concurs. "Without official guidelines, manufacturers might create clubs and balls that could make golf courses obsolete. It's important that golf remain a game of skill instead of a battle of equipment technology."

"Sort of like major league baseball outlawing aluminum bats," Kathleen comments.

WOODS

ARE THE LONGEST CLUBS IN YOUR BAG. THE 1-WOOD, OR DRIVER, IS USED TO TEE OFF ON A HOLE. WHILE FAIRWAY WOODS ARE USED TO HIT THE BALL OFF THE GROUND.

PUTTERS ARE A VERY SUBJECTIVE THING. GOLFERS ARE KNOWN TO TRY ANYTHING TO BE A GOOD PUTTER.

INCLUDING THE KITCHEN SINK!

"Exactly," Jack agrees. "At the premium level, the only real difference in clubs is marketing hype and how an individual player feels about the clubs. That's the important thing—go with what feels right for you."

"Thanks. This has been great." Kathleen shakes Tommy's hand and turns to Jack. "What's next?"

"If you're ready, we'll go to the pro shop and see if we can catch David Getbetter, our teaching professional. Perhaps he can tell you about lessons."

Kathleen smiles. "Let's strike while the iron's hot."

FIVE

A LESSON ON LESSONS

Back in the pro shop, David Getbetter stands at the counter reviewing his lesson book. He has a full schedule with fifteen lessons lined up before a playing lesson in the late afternoon. Jack explains Kathleen's situation and asks for David's help.

"Perhaps you can take a few moments to give Kathleen an overview of golf instruction," Jack says.

"Sure." David steps out from behind the counter and shakes Kathleen's hand. He's dressed in light colors. His skin has a deep tan with a few wrinkles on his forehead and around his eyes.

"So, you're a full-time teacher?" Kathleen asks.

"Yes, ma'am. Many PGA professionals specialize in a certain area of golf. Mine is teaching. That's all I do."

"And Tommy is a full-time club maker," she responds.

"That's right. We're both specialists."

"Like my tax attorney," she adds.

"Hopefully, we're not as expensive." They both laugh.

"Seriously though, I might be the biggest challenge you've ever had," Kathleen says. "Can I learn enough about golf in one month to play in a golf tournament? I know absolutely nothing, and I've never swung a golf club before."

"Sure you can. Golf's a game you can enjoy the first day you play. After learning just a few basics, you can play with anyone."

Kathleen breaks out her notepad. "I know you might not have time for a lesson today, but can you tell me where I should get golf lessons; that is, if you're not available?"

"Sure. First, you should start with a trained PGA or LPGA golf professional."

"That's important? I mean, those aren't just clubs or associations or something?"

"It's very important to you because it's a way of ensuring your professional is trained and certified. Just as you would be sure to hire a tax attorney who has passed the bar exam, you should get a lesson from someone who's professionally trained."

"That's the PGA?" she asks.

"And the LPGA, which stands for Ladies Professional Golf Association," David replies. "The PGA has more than twenty thousand members and apprentices, and the teaching division of the LPGA has over six hundred full-time teaching professionals. They're excellent teachers, and you can usually find one or more trained teachers at any golf course or driving range."

"Why can't I just get help from a friend who's a good golfer, such as Mark or Jim in my office?"

David smiles. "Actually, friends can be more of a hindrance than a help. There are certain myths about the golf swing, perpetuated by golfers, that can actually do more harm than good. You're better off ignoring most tips from friends. As well-meaning as they are, they're usually wrong. Get help from a pro."

"What's a myth about the golf swing I should know about?"

David thinks for a moment. "The all-time worst advice anyone can tell you is, 'Keep your head down.' Beginning golfers are almost always told this by well-meaning friends. In fact, keeping your head down makes it impossible to hit the ball well."

"Why?"

"Because the golf swing is not a static thing. If you lock your head down in one position, you can't swing freely and you can't move your weight through the ball. Therefore, you usually TOP it. You have to let your head move up and through the golf shot."

David demonstrates a golf swing.

"Is this the kind of thing you teach in a golf lesson?" Kathleen asks.

"Sure. Good instructors teach fundamentals. The basics of the game are quite simple:

- grip,
- STANCE,
- ALIGNMENT,
- and POSTURE.

"These are just the positions of your body prior to swinging the club. Master these, and you will have an easier time swinging the club properly."

"Well, I certainly need help. What should I do to get a lesson?"

"First, make an appointment with a professional. Second, plan on a lesson lasting a half-hour to an hour. Third, a lesson will cost anywhere from thirty dollars to two hundred dollars, depending on your pro's experience and credentials."

"Two hundred dollars!"

"Yes. Don't worry. That's not normal; but, like any other specialist, the best in the world command top dollar. You just need to find someone with whom you feel comfortable at a price you feel good about. Golf lessons are a very personal thing. You might have to shop a few pros before finding someone you feel good about. Also, you should look into taking a few video lessons."

"Video lessons?"

"Absolutely. Golf instruction can be high tech. Instructors use all kinds of teaching aids, such as video equipment, computer swing analyzers, and auditory-sensory equipment. The most common is the video camera. Watching your swing on television is a tremendous aid when learning the game. Check into a few video lessons. If nothing else, you'll have something to take home and play on the VCR."

"What should I bring to a lesson?" she asks

"An open mind and that worn-out notepad of yours," he says, laughing. "You don't even need

clubs. Most professionals will provide loaners. Just be on time and be prepared to feel a little like chopped hamburger when you're done."

"I thought this was supposed to be fun. What's so unpleasant about a lesson?"

"Most people usually get worse before they get better. That's because you learn a whole new set of SWING THOUGHTS—ideas on which to key when you swing the club. But it always works itself out, and most people improve once they practice what they've learned. Heck, even Jack Nicklaus and Arnold Palmer take lessons!"

"That's a relief," Kathleen sighs. "Can golf instructors teach me how to play and think on the course? You know, etiquette, rules, strategy . . . that sort of thing?"

"Sure. You can learn anything about the game from a good instructor. A convenient way to do this is to take lessons while on the golf course, called PLAYING LESSONS. They're usually more expensive than a regular lesson, but they can be extremely effective. In a playing lesson, the instructor and pupil play nine holes together."

"Sounds fun. But what if I want a crash course?" Kathleen inquires, pondering her short thirty-day window.

"You have several options. You can read a book or pick up some golf magazines. There are hundreds of golf instruction books out there; and, if you're diligent and studious, you can pick up a lot just by reading. Of course, books are no substitute for hands-on lessons. You might want to consider attending a golf school. A good school usually consists of a two- or three-day workshop with classroom instruction, lessons on the practice tee, and playing the golf course. It's hard work, but it's a lot of fun."

"How do I find one of these schools?" Kathleen asks.

"Ask any golf professional, or look in a golf magazine. There are all sorts of advertisements for schools around the country. Most are pretty darned good."

David begins to fidget, and Kathleen senses he's late for a lesson.

"David, thanks so much for the tips. Any parting words of wisdom?"

"Keep your head down!"

"But, I thought you said—"

"Just testing, just testing. Why don't you check with me later today, and maybe we can squeeze in your first lesson."

"Great! I'll put every myth of yours to the test."

Six

Everything but the Kitchen Sink

David leaves for his lesson, and Jack disappears to take a phone call. Turning around, Kathleen notices a young woman on the opposite side of the pro shop. Nancy Lopes, an assistant golf professional, stands behind the counter inspecting a new shipment of golf balls. An outstanding golfer and a favorite among the club's members, Nancy also is the merchandise manager at Shady Oaks, and, as Kathleen soon learns, she's a member of both the PGA and LPGA.

Nancy looks up at Kathleen standing at the counter. "You must be Kathleen, our student for the day."

"Yes," Kathleen says with a smile. "If you don't mind my asking, what are you working on?"

"Golf balls," Nancy replies. "We just received a new shipment, and I'm checking out this new decadohedron DIMPLE."

Nancy notices bewilderment on Kathleen's face and politely asks, "Do you know anything about golf balls?"

"I know absolutely nothing about golf, period."

Nancy smiles and holds up a golf ball. "This little white sphere weighs only 1.62 ounces and is 1.68 inches in diameter, but it's caused more joy and heartache over the last three hundred years than anything its size."

Kathleen smiles and opens her notepad.

"The forerunners of this decadohedron marvel date back to the early 1600s," Nancy continues. "It's a neat story. The first balls were called FEATHERIES. They were made of leather strips sewn together and stuffed with feathers."

"Feathers," Kathleen reflects as she picks up a new white golf ball. "Golf balls used to be filled with feathers!"

"Actually, the feathers were wet when they were stuffed into the ball. When they dried, they expanded and gave the ball resilience. Even the best featheries would fly only about 180 yards. That's half the distance some pros can hit one of these."

Kathleen holds up the hard white ball, examining the "decawhatever" dimples. "Technology has changed just about everything, hasn't it?"

Nancy nods. "It sure has. In the 1850s the GUTTA BALL came along. It was made from resin of the Malaysian gutta-percha tree, which made it harder than the featheries. Gutta balls remained in vogue until almost 1900 when Corburn Haskell invented the wound ball, which was the first version of today's modern ball."

"Wound ball?" Kathleen asks, looking up.

"Yes. The ball you're holding has a small liquid center with several hundred yards of rubber bands wound tightly around it. That one might have a balata or surlyn cover. I can't tell from here."

"A what cover?"

"There are two basic types of golf balls: surlyn-covered, or solid, two-piece balls; and balata-covered, wound balls. SURLYN is a man-made plastic that's harder than BALATA. Surlyn balls feel harder when you hit them, but they're also very difficult to cut when you mis-hit them."

"You mean you can cut these things?" Kathleen asks, again holding up the hard white ball.

"Sure, when you hit it with a sharp steel object such as a golf club. That's why most golfers like surlyn balls. They're tougher to cut. The downside is that surlyn balls tend to spin less, making it difficult for golfers to maneuver or curve the ball. The other kind of ball, a balata ball, has a natural rubber cover, although some of today's versions are of a man-made material. Balata is softer than surlyn, cuts easily, and is more expensive, but it also spins more, and is, therefore, easier to maneuver."

"Why does a golf ball have dimples?" Kathleen asks.

"That's an interesting story," Nancy answers. "Years ago golfers used balls with a smooth cover, but they soon discovered that balls flew better when they got nicked and cut. In no time, nicks and cuts were replaced with dimples. A ball without dimples won't fly very straight or very far."

FEATHERY GUTTA RUBBER MODERN

THERE ARE TWO TYPES OF GOLF BALLS: SURLYN-COVERED SOLID BALLS AND BALATA-COVERED WOUND BALLS. BEGINNERS SHOULD USE A SURLYN-COVERED BALL BECAUSE THEY LAST LONGER.

WOUND

SOLID
TWO PIECE

GOLF BALLS WITHOUT DIMPLES WON'T GO AS FAR AS DIMPLED BALLS.

Kathleen examines the ball in her hand more closely.

"You see, a spinning ball with dimples causes an air pressure differential around the ball—"

"Like the wing of an airplane," Kathleen interjects.

"Yes. The same principle. A well-hit ball has BACKSPIN. Along with the aerodynamic principles of dimples, backspin is what makes the ball rise and fly straight and far. Sometimes it also has SIDESPIN, which can make it curve left or right."

"That's what you mean by maneuvering the ball?"

"Yes. Those curves in a ball's flight are called HOOKS, DRAWS, SLICES, and FADES."

"You're going to have to explain those to me," Kathleen admits.

"A hook," Nancy clarifies, using her hands to demonstrate her point, "is a golf shot that curves in flight left of where you want it to go. A slice is just the opposite. It curves to the right. Both are undesirable golf shots because they travel away from your intended target. A draw, however, is a controlled curve from right to left that finishes where you want it to. A fade—likewise, a planned shot—curves slightly right toward the target.

"Of course, all these directions pertain to a right-handed player. Most golfers are right-handed, and most equipment is designed for right-handed players. If you're left-handed, however, the ball flight for hooks, slices, draws, and fades is exactly the opposite of this. Now a SHANK . . . that's something entirely different."

"I take it a shank is not a great shot."

"It's the worst shot in golf. When you hit the ball off the hosel and not off the clubface, it goes directly to the right, and it feels awful. Golfers cringe just at the mention of the word."

"Okay," Kathleen murmurs, looking again at the ball and thinking she'll have her fair share of shanks. "Let's get back to balls. How do I know what ball I need?"

"For you, it's simple," Nancy announces. "Choose a surlyn-covered, solid ball. Pros and other good players play balata-covered wound balls. You don't need them. Also, get a ninety-compression ball."

"What's that?"

"Compression is like air pressure in a tire: it's a measure of resistance. The higher the COMPRESSION, the harder the ball feels when you hit it. Manufacturers offer balls in eighty-, ninety-, or one-hundred-compression, but don't get too concerned about this. Just get ninety-compression balls. Tests show that they're all pretty much the same."

"How will I know all this?"

Nancy smiles. "Usually, ball manufacturers plaster this information on the package. If you don't know, ask the pro selling the balls. You might also consider buying used golf balls. These are balls golfers have lost in lakes and ponds. They are cheaper than new balls, and they work fine as long as they aren't cut or yellowed. You don't want to invest a lot of money in balls. You're going to lose quite a few."

"The word was 'shank,' right?" Kathleen says, chuckling as she flips the ball back to Nancy. She notices the glove display. "I suppose I'll need a pair of those, too?"

"Most likely, although golf gloves don't come in pairs. You need only one, which is usually worn on the lead hand gripping the club. Many golfers wear a glove when they play. It prevents blisters and helps you get a better grip on the club."

"Like a batting glove in baseball?"

"Same idea. Let me show you."

Nancy takes a glove and pulls it onto her left hand. "Right-handed players wear a glove on their left hand, and left-handed golfers wear one on their right."

Kathleen feels the glove. "It's very soft. What is it?"

"It's CABRETTA LEATHER, the softest leather in the world, made from a special sheepskin."

"You're kidding."

"Honest. There are two types of gloves—synthetic and leather. Synthetic material costs less and lasts longer but doesn't have the soft feel of leather."

"Yes, this feels great."

"Don't get carried away. Leather gloves are twice as expensive and don't last as long."

"I have to have one of these. Which one should I get?"

"The correct size. Gloves come in small, medium, medium-large, large, and extra-large, and each size is available in a regular or cadet model."

"Cadet?"

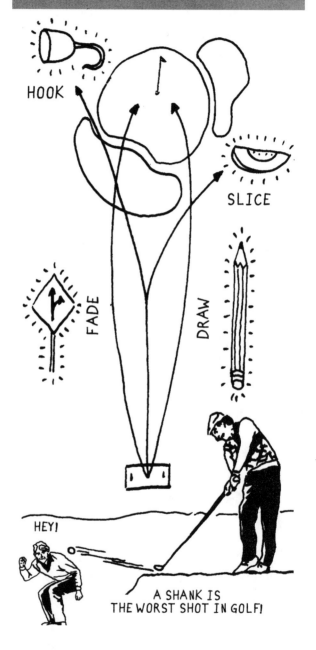

HOOK

SLICE

FADE

DRAW

HEY!

A SHANK IS
THE WORST SHOT IN GOLF!

"Yeah. The fingers are shorter on a cadet glove." Nancy looks at Kathleen's hands. "You'll probably wear a large cadet, but try several on to make sure."

"I will. While we're at it, what else do I need?"

"Do you have a golf BAG?"

Kathleen notices the golf bags lining the walls. "No. But I don't think I want to carry fourteen clubs in my hands and a bunch of golf balls in my pockets."

Nancy laughs. "In the early days of the game, that's exactly what golfers did. A caddy would carry the clubs loose. Soon somebody figured out that a small bag made life easier. As golf grew, so did the size of the bags. With most courses offering riding carts or caddies, some golf bags are large enough to hide a small family."

"Which one do I need?"

"You need a small- to medium-sized bag, maybe six to eight inches in diameter. This will carry all your clubs, about a dozen balls, a sweater, and an umbrella. If you plan to walk and carry your own bag, consider getting an even smaller bag."

"I don't have a small family yet, so how about a small one?"

"Great. And get a vinyl or canvas bag, not leather. Vinyl and canvas are cheaper, last longer, and clean easily."

"Okay, what else?"

"Do you have shoes?"

"A closetful," Kathleen admits ruefully.

"Sorry, but you might need to add another pair to your collection. Golf shoes have spikes on the bottom to give you traction and to help you stay balanced when you swing. You don't have to have a pair right away, but it's an investment you'll want to make if you plan to play golf seriously."

"And if I don't?"

"A pair of sneakers will work, but don't ever wear street shoes or heels. Street shoes will ruin a golf course. And even if you don't need golf shoes when you swing, walking up and down slippery slopes can be tricky without them."

"Okay, what else?"

"You'll need HEAD COVERS to protect your woods. They come in all shapes and colors, even cute little animal styles. You'll also need a towel, some tees, and a bag tag to identify you as the owner of your clubs. You need sunscreen. Remember, golf puts you outside in the sunshine for three or four hours at a time, and you can get sunburned on an overcast day. There are a lot of golfers who wish they had paid more attention to protecting themselves from the sun's rays while they were on the golf course. Take plenty of liquids with you, especially if you're playing in the heat of summer."

"What do you wear to play golf?" Kathleen wants to know.

"Most courses have dress codes. For men, it's usually no blue jeans, tee shirts, cutoffs, and so forth. For women, no halter tops, miniskirts, or bikini bottoms."

"Please," Kathleen responds. "Ignorant, I am. Tacky, I'm not."

Nancy laughs. "Okay, just remember, at some clubs the length of your skirt or shorts might even be measured. The fancier the club, the tougher the dress code. Just wear something comfortable, something that will allow you to swing the golf club freely."

Nancy smiles and continues, "It's gotten better with time. Seventy-five years ago, men played in coats and ties, and women played in dresses buttoned up to their chin. It wasn't much fun."

"No doubt," agrees Kathleen.

"You're learning quickly. Any questions?" Nancy asks.

"Will the test at the end of the day be essay or multiple choice?" Both laugh as Jack returns from his phone call.

"Sorry about that. I hope Nancy was able to help."

"Absolutely. I now have a long list of things I need to buy."

"Great," Jack says. "So, when you leave here, where are you going to play golf?"

"That's awfully presumptuous of you," Kathleen says, smiling.

"Maybe, but my guess is you'll be hooked before the day's over."

"If I am, where will I play? I have no idea where to go from here."

"Unfortunately, I have a few more things to do, so I'd like you to meet with our membership director,

Betsy Kingston," Jack says. "She'd like to have lunch with you in the grillroom and tell you all about places to play. How does that sound?"

"Like a double eagle with a decadohedron."

SEVEN

WHERE TO TEE IT UP

In the grillroom during lunch, Kathleen begins to feel at home at Shady Oaks.

Betsy Kingston, the club's membership director, is a professionally dressed woman in her early forties with shoulder-length hair and a light tan. Kathleen introduces herself and gives a quick synopsis of her day at Shady Oaks and her plight as a golf novice. Betsy is very understanding. After the food arrives, Kathleen asks Betsy the next question on her list.

"Given that I have only one month to learn this game, where do I play and practice?" she asks. "This is the first golf course I've ever been to."

Betsy takes a sip of tea and begins. "To practice, you will need to find a DRIVING RANGE or a course that has a driving range. That's where you can hit all the balls you want without having to pick them up. You can get either a bag or bucket of balls and practice what you've learned. Most golf courses, whether PRIVATE or PUBLIC, have ranges."

"Should I join a private club?"

"Maybe, but only if you become serious about the game. Usually, you have to be invited or sponsored by a member. Once they accept you as a candidate, you pay what's known as an INITIATION FEE. That's an up-front fee that can range from one hundred dollars to one hundred thousand dollars depending on the quality of the club."

"Do you get it back if you leave?"

"It depends on the club. Sometimes the initiation fee is refundable. Sometimes the fee gives you equity, or ownership, in the club. Even that can be wholly or partially refundable."

"What are the advantages of a private club?" Kathleen asks.

"For some people, it's a status thing; for others, it's an attractive social setting. Most people join private clubs because they enjoy having their own course on which to play without having to fight the kind of crowds often found at public or municipal courses."

Kathleen thinks of her health-club membership. "Do you also pay dues?"

"Yes. Most clubs charge monthly dues that pay the operational costs of running a club."

"Are there any other charges?"

"Again, it depends on the club. Most clubs will require you to pay for things such as cart fees, caddy fees, meals, and range balls. It can add up."

"Sounds expensive," Kathleen says.

"Private clubs can be expensive. Many people prefer to play at a public golf course."

"Which, I guess, anyone can play?"

"Correct. There are many public golf courses where you can play at reasonable rates."

"Public courses don't have initiation fees and dues, do they?"

"Right again. But when you play at a public golf course, you pay a GREEN FEE. That's the fee charged to play the course, like a rental charge or usage fee."

"And how much does a green fee usually cost?"

"It depends on the course. Generally, the nicer the golf course, the higher the fee. It also depends on when you play. On weekends, when everybody wants to play, the rates are usually higher than they are on weekdays."

"Does the green fee include the use of a golf cart?"

"No. But many golf courses allow you to walk, thus giving you the option of not having to pay a cart fee. If you do ride, or if the course requires you to take a cart, you pay a CART FEE. It's like renting a car for a round of golf."

Kathleen considers her options. "Are public golf courses busy? Sounds like they should be."

"Usually quite busy. Competition for a time to play can be intense. At some public courses, golfers get in line at three in the morning three or four days ahead of time for a chance to play."

"This gal might be out at three in the morning, but I can assure you it won't be to play golf!"

Betsy laughs. "That just shows you how enthusiastic some people are about the game. Another thing you should know is that public courses aren't always in the best condition, and sometimes the LAYOUT, or design, isn't quite as good as you would find at, say, a country club. In some cases, these municipal courses—often referred to as 'munis' [MYOO-neez]—are operated by a municipality short on both money and manpower, and the courses suffer somewhat. This isn't always the case. There are some excellent public golf courses. Pebble Beach, for example, in Monterey, California, is a public course."

Still pondering her choices, Kathleen says, "As much as I hate to admit it, I'm something of a snob. What if I want to play at a nice course but don't want to join a private club?"

"Then play at a DAILY FEE or a RESORT course."

"Daily fee?"

"That's right. A daily fee course is, in essence, a course open to anyone, but this term is used by golfers because these courses are usually better designed and in better condition than typical public or municipal courses. Daily fee or resort courses usually cost more but on the whole they're worth it. Many are as nice as private clubs."

"And I guess resort courses are found at places such as Palm Springs?" Kathleen asks.

"Yes. Major resort areas such as Hilton Head, Palm Beach, Orlando, Palm Springs, and Las Vegas have plenty of golf courses. Generally, they're great courses, very well maintained, and very expensive."

Kathleen and Betsy work on their salads.

"Another type of course," Betsy adds, "is a SEMI-PRIVATE golf club, which does a little of everything.

These clubs have members, but they also allow some public play. There are usually restrictions on the public, but these are good, well-maintained golf courses."

"Okay, let's go back to the beginning," Kathleen says. "You said most clubs or courses have driving ranges or practice tees?"

"Most. But you should also look for a freestanding driving range—one without a golf course attached. Many have miniature golf, video games, and the like. Make sure you find one with lights for evening use, good balls, and grass to hit off. Some ranges use artificial turf, which makes it difficult to learn the game correctly."

"You mean Astroturf?"

"Right, like a football field. But find one with real-grass teeing areas. You will play off real grass, so you should practice on real grass."

They finish their grilled chicken salads, then Betsy asks, "Do you have a better idea about where to play now?"

"I do for at least the next thirty days. We'll see after that."

"That's great," Betsy replies. "If you've learned that much, I feel my day has been a success. I've got to get back to my office, and Jack expects you back in the golf shop. I think he wants to introduce you to Mr. Boatwater, one of our more colorful members. He can tell you about the rules of golf, if you don't mind listening to a few stories in the process."

Kathleen smiles. "I don't mind at all. Thanks for everything, Betsy. You have been a great help."

"You're quite welcome. Good luck at your outing."

"Thanks. I'm going to need it."

TYPES OF GOLF COURSES

1. PUBLIC— A COURSE ANYONE CAN PLAY.

2. DAILY FEE— TERM FOR A VERY GOOD PUBLIC COURSE.

3. PRIVATE— A COURSE OPEN TO MEMBERS AND THEIR GUESTS ONLY.

4. SEMIPRIVATE— A PRIVATE CLUB THAT ALLOWS LIMITED PUBLIC PLAY.

5. RESORT— A COURSE AT A VACATION SPOT OPEN TO THE PUBLIC.

EIGHT

THE GREAT EQUALIZER

Lunch was delicious, and Kathleen feels refreshed. She hasn't learned this much in one day since college. As she enters the pro shop, she notices a bulletin board on the wall.

Jack steps out of his office. "How ya doin' so far?"

"Pretty good, I guess." Looking at the board, she notices upcoming tournament announcements and a sign announcing handicaps with a list of names below it.

"Do handicapped people play golf?"

"Excuse me?" Jack asks.

Kathleen points to the board. "There seems to be a disproportionate number of handicapped people playing golf here."

Jack laughs. "Actually, that refers to a different kind of handicap. Don't get me wrong, some disabled people do play golf, but that's not what a golf handicap is all about. Actually, handicaps are a critical part of the game."

"How can a handicap be good?"

"It's not what you think," Jack assures her. "A HANDICAP is a mathematical equalizer, a compensation in strokes given to golfers based on their past performances. Handicaps enable golfers with different abilities to compete on equal terms. They level the playing field."

"Please explain," Kathleen asks.

"Okay, when you were a kid, did you ever play pickup games—basketball, baseball, or even football?" Jack asks.

"Sure, we had street games all the time."

"All right, remember when one team was better than the other? What you probably did was spot the team with less ability a few points, or a couple of runs. Rather than starting at zero, you might spot the less-talented team two, four, or even more points, depending on how bad the other team was."

"Sure," Kathleen remembers. "I was always on the receiving end of those spots."

"Then you can understand the basic premise of a handicap in golf. If all four hundred members at this club played against one another, there would be no way for everyone to spot everyone else. There would be too many combinations. Handicaps take care of that.

"For example, let's say you and an imaginary friend have established handicaps. Your handicap is ten, and your friend's is twenty. You both play. Your friend shoots 90 and you shoot an 81."

"I win."

"Ah, that's the beauty of handicaps," Jack says. "Because you have a handicap of ten and your friend has a handicap of twenty, you have, in essence, spotted her ten shots. While your GROSS score is actually better than hers, your NET score is not. You have a net 71, but your friend has a net score of 70."

"So she wins?"

"That's right, she beats you by one stroke because of her handicap."

"How do you know I should be giving her ten shots? I mean, there are four hundred golfers at Shady Oaks, right? How do you know who gives strokes and who receives strokes?"

"By obtaining an official USGA handicap. And you do that by posting your golf scores at a golf club or with a local golf association."

Kathleen makes notes as Jack continues.

"The USGA has a complicated formula for computing handicaps known as GHIN. That's an acronym for GOLF HANDICAP INFORMATION NETWORK. It's the most widely used golf handicapping system in the country."

"My friend and I couldn't just figure our own handicaps and spot each other accordingly?" Kathleen suggests.

"Sure you could. But if you want to play in a tournament, you would need a USGA-sanctioned handicap. In fact, the spotting scenario you just described is how most weekend games of golf are set up. Friends get together, each knows what the other is likely to shoot, and they spot strokes accordingly."

"But to play in a tournament, I need a handicap?"

"Depending on the type of event, yes," Jack clarifies.

"And you get one by posting scores?" Kathleen continues.

"Right. After every eighteen-hole round you play, you should post your score on the handicap board. After you've posted a certain number of rounds, you'll be given a handicap that will periodically change as your scores change."

Kathleen looks back at the computer printout of handicaps with its seemingly endless names and numbers.

"How do you know golfers are posting their actual scores and not fudging to get a better handicap?"

"That's a good question. The answer is that some golfers do fudge a little. This works for a while, but eventually these people are exposed and earn the label SANDBAGGERS, a reputation you don't want."

"Why not just call them 'cheaters'?"

"Basically, we do. In golf parlance, sandbagging is synonymous with cheating. Sandbaggers are usually reprimanded by their club or local golf association if their friends don't get to them first. It isn't as big a problem as you might think. Golf is a game of high integrity, so most people post their true scores—all of them, good and bad."

Kathleen scribbles in her notepad. "Can you take your handicap anywhere and use it in a tournament?"

"Anywhere in the country, but this is where it gets a little complicated," Jack says.

"You mean it's not complicated now?"

Jack laughs. "I guess you're right. Even I don't understand it all. You only need to know a few more basics, however. First, remember that all golf courses are different. Some are difficult; some easy. If you have a handicap established at a course that's easy, and you take that handicap to another course that's very hard, you'll be at a disadvantage. That's why the USGA devised two factors—COURSE RATING and SLOPE INDEX. Both of these take into account the differences in golf courses and the differences in golfers."

"What do I need to know about them?" Kathleen asks.

"You don't necessarily need to know how they're computed, but you need to know how to use them. You'll usually find the course rating posted somewhere at the club, if not on the scorecard. It's usually a number around par for the course and it's measured to a decimal point. For example, the par for a golf course might be 72, and the course rating might be 74.4. That rating refers to what a SCRATCH, or zero-handicap, golfer would normally score on that particular course."

"That would be a hard golf course," Kathleen observes.

"That's right. If the par is 72 and the course rating is 69.1, that would be considered a fairly easy course. For the beginner, however, none of them seems easy."

Kathleen laughs, then asks, "Why do I need to know the course rating?"

Jack explains that course ratings allow people who travel and play golf while on the road to take their scores from different courses all over the country and post those scores back at their home club in order to establish a handicap. He also explains that the second factor, the slope index, is a measure of the relative difficulty of each golf course. Both ratings are complicated, and Jack emphasizes that Kathleen shouldn't try to understand how they are calculated. All she needs to know is that the USGA works hard to make handicaps equitable for all golfers, even if a few players get confused along the way.

Glancing once again at the board on the wall, Kathleen sees several notices for upcoming tournaments.

"What about tournaments? Are handicaps used in all tournaments?"

"Not all," Jack replies. "The most basic golf tournament, in fact, is a low-gross tournament. It's pretty simple. Everybody plays and the golfer with the lowest score wins. That's the kind of event you see the pros play.

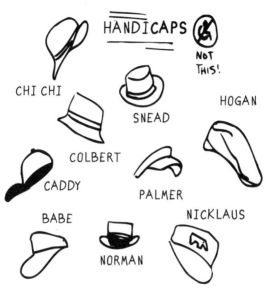

"The most common handicapped event is the LOW-NET tournament. Everybody plays and the golfer with the lowest score, after subtracting his or her handicap, wins. Since handicaps are golf's great equalizer, golfers of all skill levels can compete in a low-net event."

"What about the tournament I'm playing in next month?" she asks. "It's a scrabble, whatever that means."

Jack laughs. "You mean scramble."

"Yes, that's it. A scramble!"

"That's one of the most common events for golf outings. A SCRAMBLE, sometimes referred to as a captain's choice or a FORT LAUDERDALE, is an easy and fun tournament for large groups. The people you play with are a team, and your team is playing against every other team. On the first hole, you and your teammates hit your TEE SHOTS. The team then selects the best shot, everyone else picks up his or her ball, and then all golfers hit from the preferred spot. You continue this process, shot after shot, until the hole is completed. Then on the next hole, everybody hits, the best shot is picked, you hit from there, and so on, and so on."

"That does sound fun, although I doubt my shot will ever be the one used."

"You'd be surprised. If you hit a bad shot in a scramble, it's okay. Scramble teams usually consist of four or even five golfers, meaning you get four or five chances each time at hitting a really good shot. Somebody else on your team will usually hit a good one. It's a great format for beginners. In fact, I've seen total beginners sink birdie and par putts that have saved their team. That's what makes it a great format. Everybody contributes."

Kathleen feels great relief. "What are some other formats?"

"Other common matches include the NASSAU, in which a match is divided into three parts—front nine, back nine, and overall eighteen. In the STABLE-FORD, points are assigned for various scores on a hole; and in the BEST BALL, partners play as a team, with the best score on a hole counting as the team score."

Kathleen remarks, "There's a lot more to golf than I had thought."

Jack agrees and continues, "There are as many different golf games as there are golfers. That's one of the things that makes golf such a great game. You can play any kind of match you want and, believe me, golfers are a very imaginative group."

As she finishes her notes, Kathleen notices a stately gentleman in golf attire entering the shop. He picks up a club and grips it as though he's going to hit a shot right there in the pro shop.

"Ah, there's P. J., the member I wanted you to meet," Jack says as he walks over to the gentleman.

"I know absolutely nothing about golf," Kathleen confides, extending her hand after Jack introduces them.

"Is that so?" P. J. Boatwater says. "It's a great game and one I'm sure you'll learn to love."

Jack puts his hand on P. J.'s shoulder. "I was hoping you could spend a few minutes teaching Kathleen a few basic rules of golf."

The gentleman's eyes light up. As Jack expected, this is no problem for P. J. Boatwater. "I'd be happy to help this fine young lady," he replies.

NINE

THE RULES OF THE ROAD

"So, you'd like to know the rules of golf," P. J. Boatwater remarks as he pulls a pipe from his back pocket and fills it with sweet-smelling tobacco.

"Yes, indeed; I'm trying to learn all I can," Kathleen explains.

"Wonderful, my favorite kind of student," he replies, lighting the pipe and pausing for effect. "The rules aren't etched in stone. Like most rules or laws, they're subject to constant review and revision. Even though there are only thirty-four rules of golf, the interpretations and applications can be so complicated that even the pros call for a rules official when there's a question about the rules."

"Great, do I need to carry my cellular phone with me to the course?"

"No," P. J. laughs. "But the most important equipment you need after clubs, balls, and a bag is an updated rules book."

"If there are only thirty-four rules, why are they so complicated?" she asks.

"Because you can't imagine how many different situations golfers put themselves in. That's why we have a book of decisions on the rules of golf."

"Decisions?" she queries.

"Sure, think of it like our judicial system. The rule book is the constitution. It's a simple document that outlines the way we play the game. The decisions, handed down by the USGA and the R&A, are like court decisions. They deal with actual situations that have occurred, such as a ball landing in a bird's nest or a clubhead coming off in the middle of a swing."

"Tell her the Arnold Palmer story," Jack says.

"Oh, I'm sure she doesn't want to hear—"

"Oh, I do," Kathleen pleads.

P. J. smiles and puffs on his pipe. "Years ago I was a rules official at the U.S. Open. Arnold Palmer hit his ball into the sand trap of the hole I was officiating. Suddenly, I saw Arnie thrashing around in the sand trap, sand going everywhere. It was a mess. Of course, there's a rule that prohibits you from touching the sand in a trap before you swing, so this thrashing around was a violation and should have resulted in a penalty."

"Of course," Kathleen agrees, as if she knows what she's talking about.

"So I went over to the trap, and there's Arnie holding up a four-foot rattlesnake on the end of his sand wedge. He looked up at me and called out, 'It was him or me, P. J. How you gonna rule?' "

P. J. laughs as if it's the first time he has told this story.

"What did you do?" Kathleen asks.

"We made a ruling right on the spot. We decided protecting oneself from bodily harm wasn't a rules violation, even if Arnie did dig up half the sand trap in the process." He laughs again.

"Wow!" Kathleen exclaims. "I guess truth *is* stranger than fiction!"

"You bet," P. J. affirms. "But don't worry, the basic rules of golf aren't difficult to learn. In fact, they're fairly easy."

"Okay, try me," Kathleen says.

"All right. The most basic axiom of golf is to hit the ball, find it, and hit it again. Play the ball as you find it, play the course as you find it, and when it's not possible to do either, do what's fair."

Kathleen retrieves her notepad and begins writing.

P. J. continues. "You're allowed to tee up the ball when you start each hole, but other than that, you must play the ball as it lies, or as you find it. The only time you can touch your ball is on the green. Once there, you can mark the position of your ball with a small object. I advise using a coin. Pick up the ball, clean it, and replace it on the same spot."

"Keep going," Kathleen urges.

P. J. does just that. He tells her that, while most of the time you play the ball as it LIES, there are some special exceptions when a player may improve the lie. Usually, these exceptions are allowed in cases involving bad weather conditions, construction, or other extenuating circumstances. He also explains that, although you can't move your ball, you can re-move LOOSE IMPEDIMENTS. These include pine-cones, leaves, twigs, beer cans, and stones. The only two stipulations to the loose impediment rule are that the impediments must be around your ball, and they cannot be fixed or growing. You may not, for example, dig a stone out of the ground or break a limb off a tree.

"What about those hazards you were talking about earlier?" she inquires.

P. J. nods and goes on. "You can play your ball from a hazard such as a pond or a stream if you can find it. Water hazards are defined by red or yellow lines or stakes. You can't touch the hazard with your club before you swing. If you do, you've GROUNDED your club and that's a penalty. If you can't play your ball from a hazard, you may, under penalty of one stroke, drop the ball or a new ball outside the hazard."

"Are you penalized every time you want to move your ball?" Kathleen asks.

"Not always. Sometimes you're allowed free RELIEF, such as when your ball comes to rest near or on an artificial obstruction, such as a sprinkler head or cart path, or if your ball has come to rest in an area deemed to be GROUND UNDER REPAIR. In these cases you may DROP the ball away from the condi-tion that allows relief but not nearer the hole. When you drop the ball, you hold it at arm's length, shoul-der high, and drop it."

"Even I can do that," she concedes. "What if my ball is in someone's backyard? Is that a hazard?"

"No. That's almost always OUT OF BOUNDS, which are those areas of the golf course marked by white stakes beyond which you may not play. If your ball goes out of bounds, you must return to the spot where you last hit it, add a penalty stroke to your score, and hit again."

"That sounds bad."

"It's not fun, particularly the part about walking back to where you hit the last shot—unless, of course, you hit a provisional ball."

"A what?"

"A provisional ball. If you suspect your ball is out of bounds or lost, you may immediately hit a second ball, or PROVISIONAL BALL. If you then discover that your first ball is actually out of bounds or lost, you may proceed with the provisional ball, adding a penalty stroke. In this case, your tee shot with a provisional ball would count as your third stroke, and so forth. This saves walking back to the point where the first shot was struck."

"Okay, I'm with you so far. What else do I need to know so I won't embarrass myself?"

"You can't have more than fourteen clubs in your bag."

Kathleen knows this, but writes it down anyway.

"You can't ask your opponent for advice that's not public knowledge, such as, 'What club did you hit?' or 'Which way did your putt break?' But you may ask, 'How long is this hole?' or 'Is that out of bounds over there?' It's a complicated rule partly because golfers are so darned nice they want to help everybody."

"I can't imagine anyone wanting advice from me, anyway," she comments.

P. J. smiles. "You and your fellow players can't agree to waive the rules just because you don't like them. That will result in DISQUALIFICATION for everyone involved."

"Like getting thrown out of a baseball game?"

"Right. Breaking certain rules, such as signing an incorrect scorecard or making a mistake and not rectifying it, results in disqualification."

"Wow! What *can* I do?" Kathleen blurts out.

"You can move your ball if it's in a burrowing-animal hole. You can move your ball if it's in CASUAL WATER, or standing water, from a rainfall or a broken sprinkler. You can replace your ball if another player hits it by mistake. However, the player who hit the wrong ball is penalized. And you can replace your ball if it's moved or taken by an OUTSIDE AGENCY, such as a dog. So you see, golf's really fair. It's just complicated at times."

"Are there other rules I need to know?"

"Yes. You need to know all of them but only the basics of each rule. You could spend your whole life studying the nuances of each rule, like I have. All you need to do is get a rule book and have it handy in case you get stuck."

"I will. Thanks, P. J. This has been quite an education."

"Any time. What's next on your agenda?"

At that moment Jack comes back out of his office and answers the question. "I'm taking her to meet Elmer. He's going to cover golf etiquette."

"There's no better teacher than Elmer Post," P. J. observes. "Tell you what, I'm headed out that way. If you don't mind my company a little longer, I'll take you out and introduce you."

"Thanks, P. J.," Jack says as he opens the door for them.

P. J. leads Kathleen out of the pro shop and down a small concrete stairway leading to the back of the clubhouse building.

Outside in the caddy pen are several young men dressed in white jumpsuits with towels draped over their shoulders.

"Is Elmer around?" P. J. asks.

"Yes, sir, Mr. Boatwater," one of the boys replies as he runs off to find Mr. Post.

A moment later an elderly gentleman sporting a tie and touring cap steps into the caddy pen. "P. J., how are you?"

"Fine, Elmer, fine. Look, Elmer, I'd like you to meet Kathleen. She's trying to learn a little about our fine game, and I've told her all I know about the rules of golf."

"That was an easy lesson, wasn't it?" Elmer laughs, extending his hand to Kathleen.

"I'm afraid P. J.'s setting you up, Mr. Post," Kathleen says. "I know absolutely nothing about golf, and I've got a short time to learn."

"We were hoping you could fill her in on the finer points of golf etiquette," P. J. says.

"Of course, of course," Elmer says, motioning Kathleen to follow him to a bench in the shade. "My caddies tell me I talk too much, so bear with me."

TEN

BEHAVE YOURSELF

Elmer and Kathleen sit on a bench and look across the parking lot. "You know, I've been here thirty-one years and I've brought a lot of kids through our caddy program," Elmer says. "I might not have created a lot of great golfers, but hopefully I've fostered a few gentlemen. I can't think of any sport other than golf with a higher code of conduct."

"From what I've heard so far, I gather that golf's integrity and etiquette go hand in hand," Kathleen says.

"Absolutely. Basic golf etiquette and decorum are not hard to learn. Why don't we start with the basics?"

Kathleen opens her well-worn notepad.

"First of all, you need to know that golf is played with one to four players in a group. While it's possible to play by yourself as a single, most courses require you to play in a group of four known as a FOURSOME. If you don't have a group, most courses will pair you with other golfers to form one."

"You mean people you don't know?"

"Sure. Golfers are a social lot. It's not uncommon for golfers to join a club without knowing a single person. Playing golf is how they meet fellow members and make friends."

"What's the procedure for making a reservation?"

"A TEE TIME," Elmer says, correcting her.

"Yes, a tee time. How do I make one?"

"If you have a group, that is a THREESOME or a foursome already set up, all you do is call the golf course and schedule a day and time. Some courses don't require tee times, but it's always a good idea to call ahead. As a rule, most courses won't allow singles to schedule tee times. Just show up and they'll pair you with a TWOSOME or a threesome."

"Once on the course, you must adhere to some important rules. First, when you're on the tee, the first person to hit is said to have the HONOR. On the first tee, the honor is determined by a coin toss or mutual agreement. Every hole thereafter, the person with the lowest gross score on the previous hole has the honor and therefore tees off first. The second person to tee off was the one with the second-lowest score, and so on."

"What about other shots? How do you know when it's your turn to hit?" Kathleen inquires.

"Simple. The golfer who is farthest from the hole is AWAY and plays first. It's important to stand well behind or to the side of the player hitting and to remain absolutely quiet and still. Sometimes this procedure is ignored, and golfers play ready golf. They hit when they're ready and it's safe. This speeds play and is fine when you are playing with people you know well. Of course, as a beginner, you must remember to count all your strokes, even the whiffs."

"The whats?" Kathleen asks.

"The WHIFFS," Elmer repeats. "That's when you swing and miss. Believe me, you will have more than a few of those in your early stages of this game. You must count them. They are strokes.

"Next, after you have played your shot from the fairway, you should replace your DIVOT."

"Divot?" Kathleen echoes.

"That's the large piece of grass or turf sometimes unearthed by the club when it hits the ball. Divots should be replaced and stepped on lightly."

"Will the grass grow back?"

"In some instances, yes. But replacing it is more a service to your fellow golfer. Nothing is worse than hitting a good shot only to find it at the bottom of a divot. Remember, we play the ball as it lies."

"Yes," Kathleen states. "P. J. was quite adamant about that."

"Good. Now the same is true in a sand trap. After you hit the ball, you should always smooth the sand with a rake, leaving the BUNKER as you found it. Never leave footprints in a sand trap, and never walk out of the steep side of a sand bunker."

"What about other parts of the course?"

"There are some very important guidelines for you to follow once you are on the green. For starters, you should remain still and quiet when someone is putting. You should never stand in the line of someone's putt."

"The line?"

"Yes, the LINE is his or her intended path of the ball to the hole. Remember, putting requires that the ball roll along a smooth surface. If you step in someone's line, the grass might not be quite as smooth and the putt not as true.

"Also, be conscious of your shadow. You might be out of a player's sight, but your shadow could be looming over the hole or the player's line of play. This is very annoying and is something you should always avoid."

Kathleen scribbles.

"When someone is putting and the distance is such that the golfer can't see the hole, you should ATTEND THE FLAGSTICK. It's against the rules for a putted ball to hit the flagstick. In order for the player to see the hole and not break the rule, you might be asked to stand quietly and hold the flagstick until the player strokes the putt, then you should remove it quickly and lay it aside."

"Can I lay the flagstick on the green?" she inquires.

"Yes, but gently. Remember, greens are a delicate surface."

Elmer pauses to allow Kathleen to finish writing.

"Here's a very important point: Always repair your ball mark on the green. Always."

"Is that like a divot?" she asks.

"No. A BALL MARK is the small hole or indentation made when your ball lands on the green. Repair the mark using a golf tee, inserting it at an angle under the indentation and pressing forward so as to push the earth over the depression. Once it's covered, gently tap the mark with your putter or your foot to smooth any irregularities."

"Won't the grass grow back anyway?" Kathleen asks.

"Yes, but an unrepaired ball mark might take a week to heal, making for an eyesore and putting a hindrance on what's normally a beautiful grass surface."

Kathleen writes and Elmer waits. Mr. Post prefers to lecture than to engage in lengthy conversation, which is obviously a trait he picked up from years of training kids to be caddies. Kathleen doesn't mind.

"Let's talk about the pace of play," he continues. "You should always try to play as fast as possible. A round of golf for a foursome playing eighteen holes should take no more than four and a half hours, preferably less. Slow play is the bane of golf, and there's nothing that will irritate your fellow golfers more than having to wait on you."

"But if I'm a beginner, won't I be too slow?"

Elmer explains that even the worst players can play at an acceptable pace. Some tips for speeding play include:

- Be ready when it's your time to hit.
- Don't wait to select your club or walk to your ball.
- Don't stand on the green and count your

score. Walk briskly to the next hole and calculate your score along the way.

- If your group is playing slower than the group directly behind you, stop, step aside, and allow the faster group to PLAY THROUGH.

Elmer also explains the rules of safety concerning the use of golf carts:

- Never drive a cart on or near a green or teeing area.
- Never drive a cart through a hazard such as a sand trap.
- Before exiting the cart, make sure the brake is properly engaged and locked.
- Avoid sudden starts and stops.
- Never park a cart on an incline.

These all seem very sensible to Kathleen. She looks up from her notepad. A group of caddies is listening. Their looks suggest they've heard Elmer's lectures before.

Elmer continues. "Let's talk safety. Never walk in front of someone about to play, and never hit until the golfers in front of you are well out of range. If you take a practice swing, make sure it's clear around you. Many golfers have been injured by simply not paying attention."

"What if you accidentally hit a ball at someone?" she asks.

"Then you yell 'FORE!' as loud as you can. This is golf vernacular for 'Look out!' If someone yells 'Fore!' in your direction, bend over and put your hands on top of your head."

"Do people often get hit by golf balls?" she asks.

"Not often, but it does happen and it can be serious. Caution is always the best course while on the course, I always say."

This brings a collective groan from the eavesdropping caddies who have obviously heard all of Elmer's sayings before.

Elmer ignores them and presses on with some other points of note:

- Never place your golf bag on a green.
- Never drag your feet at any time, particularly when wearing spikes and when on the putting green.
- In the event that you ever see lightning on the golf course, suspend play and return to the clubhouse immediately! More people are killed on the golf course by lightning than die in hurricanes, tornadoes, and floods combined.

Upon hearing all this, Kathleen raises her eyebrows but says nothing.

"Always conduct yourself in as reserved a manner as possible," Elmer continues. "No shouting or carrying on: this is a genteel game. But, of course, you know all this."

He smiles and wipes his brow. "I've been teaching kids too long."

"Thanks for the vote of confidence, but I didn't know that," Kathleen admits. "The only thing I'm still a little uncomfortable with are all the golf terms. People here and in my office use them so easily. I've got to tell you, it sounds like a foreign language."

DON'T WALK IN FRONT OF ANYONE,
AND DON'T HIT WHEN SOMEONE IS
IN FRONT OF YOU. IF YOU DO HIT
NEAR SOMEONE, YELL "FORE!"
THAT'S GOLF FOR "WATCH OUT!"

Elmer chuckles. "Yes, golfers have a way of doing that. The game has a language all its own."

He reaches into his pocket and pulls out a worn pamphlet with creased edges.

"This is the glossary I give to all my caddies. I compiled it almost twenty years ago, and I update it every two years as new terms come along. It might not include everything, but there's enough here for you to engage in a conversation about golf."

Kathleen takes the pamphlet (see chapter 12) and leafs through it. "Thank you so much, Mr. Post. This has been a wonderful help. Even if I shoot one million, at least I won't embarrass myself."

"Nonsense. You go out there and kick their rears."

"Mr. Post, that doesn't sound very gentleman-like."

Elmer laughs. "I said we behaved properly on the course. That doesn't mean we don't compete like the devil to win. Now go out there and show those buggers what you've got."

They both laugh heartily, get up from the bench, and head back into the clubhouse.

THOU SHALT REPAIR
THY BALL MARKS

THOU SHALT REPLACE
THY DIVOTS

THOU SHALT RAKE
THY FOOTPRINTS IN
A SAND TRAP (BUNKER)

THOU SHALT BE
STILL AND QUIET
WHEN SOMEONE IS
HITTING

THOU SHALT NOT
WALK IN THE LINE
OF SOMEONE'S PUTT

THOU SHALT NEVER
DRIVE A GOLF CART
NEAR A GREEN

THOU SHALT NEVER
PUT THY BAG DOWN OR
DRAG THY FEET ON A
GREEN

THOU SHALT NOT HIT
UNTIL GOLFERS IN
FRONT ARE OUT OF
RANGE

THOU SHALT NEVER
PLAY AT A SLOW PACE

THOU SHALT LET
FASTER PLAYERS
PLAY THROUGH

Eleven

Meeting the Challenge

Kathleen, who now knows a lot about golf, straightens her scarf as she opens the door to her twenty-fifth-floor office.

It will be a busy week. Another proposal for a potentially lucrative account is overdue, and she still has to follow up on several proposals sent out last week. Three new clients have signed on in the last few weeks and if one more proposal is accepted, she might have to add staff and increase office space.

After a quick check of her message box, she walks down the hallway to the office kitchen for her first cup of strong black coffee. Mark and Jim are there, as usual, talking about the weekend.

"He threw them all in the lake?" Mark asks.

"Every last one of them. He started with the driver and worked his way down, one at a time, whirling them like helicopters."

"What did you do?"

"I just stood there. When he got down to the last club, I unstrapped his bag and handed it to him."

"No, you didn't!"

"I did. I gave him the bag, and he heaved it in with them."

Jim is holding his side, laughing hysterically.

"But, no, that's not the best part. His car keys were in the golf bag. He had to take off his pants and wade into the lake to find them."

Jim is no longer making noise. Laughter has drained all the breath out of him and his face is bloodred.

"What on earth are you two talking about now?" Kathleen asks.

"Oh, I had another interesting golf game this past weekend," Mark says. Jim is still holding his sides, laughing uncontrollably. "By the way, how did your outing go yesterday with Mr. Davis?"

She smiles. Over the past month she's played ten rounds, practiced at the range daily, and met more new people than she normally would in a year.

"We had a scratch player on our team using one of those titanium drivers. He just ripped it off of every tee. We came to the last hole, a par-five, needing eagle to win. So he just cranks it and we end up less than 150 from the DANCE FLOOR. Of course, everybody either shanks or tops their shot, leaving me with a five-wood to this elevated green. . . ."

Mark and Jim stand amazed. What on earth has happened to Kathleen? Then it slowly dawns on them. They now have a boss who plays golf, and Monday mornings are never going to be the same!

TWELVE

ELMER'S GLOSSARY

ace. A hole in one.

address. The position taken by a golfer when preparing to start a swing or stroke.

alignment. Preshot body positioning. One of the fundamentals in instruction.

approach. A shot from off the green aimed at getting close to the hole.

apron. The low-cut grassy area surrounding a green, cut shorter than the fairway and almost as short as the green.

arc. The near-circular curve around the body made by swinging the club.

attend the flagstick. Holding the flagstick to mark the position of the hole while a fellow competitor putts.

away. Being the golfer farthest from the hole who is next to play.

back nine. The second nine holes of an eighteen-hole golf course.

backspin. The reverse spin imparted to a ball by the clubhead, making the ball fly higher and farther, and stop quicker on the green.

bag. A vinyl, leather, or canvas bag for carrying clubs, balls, and accessories.

balata. A natural or synthetic rubber material used for the cover of a golf ball, preferred by professional and low-handicap golfers.

ball mark. The indentation in turf made when a lofted shot lands on the putting green.

bent grass. The finest grass available for use on golf greens and on some fairways, found primarily in northern climates.

bermuda grass. A coarsely textured grass used where bent grass will not grow, different varieties of which are used on fairways, tees, and greens.

best ball (better ball). The best score on a hole by two or more partners in a best-ball match.

birdie. A score of one under par on a hole.

bite. When a ball lands and stops nearly dead with little roll.

blast. To play a ball out of the sand.

bogey. A score of one over par on a hole.

break. The curve in a putt due to slope in a green. A player allows for the break, sometimes referred to as the BORROW.

bunker. A sand trap or grassy depression from which it is difficult to play.

cabretta leather. A soft leather made from a special sheepskin, used in the manufacture of golf gloves.

caddy. A person who carries a player's clubs and helps him or her with club selection and course strategy.

caddy master. An employee of a golf course who manages the caddies and assigns them to golfers.

cart fee. The rental fee paid for using a golf cart during a round.

casual water. Standing water on a course, not part of a hazard, from which you may take relief without penalty.

cavity back. Design of iron club with concave back. Generally believed to be easier to hit and more forgiving for beginners.

chilidip. A poor chip shot that usually travels only a few feet.

chip (chip shot). A short, lofted shot from around the green.

chip in. To hole out or sink your chip shot.

chole. A Belgian game thought to be a forerunner of golf.

club. Any of various instruments used to hit a golf ball, including woods, irons, and putters.

clubface. The hitting portion of the clubhead, usually featuring grooves or scoring.

clubhead. The portion of the club, opposite the grip, designed for striking the ball.

club length. The length of a golf club, often used to measure distances on the course for rules purposes.

collar. The closely mown area surrounding the green that buffers the green from the fairway or rough.

compression. A golf ball's resistance to being hit, normally expressed in units of eighty-, ninety-, or one-hundred-compression.

course rating. A calculation of a course's difficulty used in handicapping.

cup. The plastic container inside the hole that holds the flagstick in place.

daily fee course. An upscale public facility.

dance floor. Slang for the green, or putting surface.

dimple. One of the hundreds of rounded depressions on a golf ball that make it fly higher, truer, and farther.

disqualification. A rules violation that results in being removed from a competition.

divot. The turf cut from the ground when a ball is hit.

dogleg. The sharp bend in the fairway of a golf hole.

double bogey. A score of two over par on a hole.

double eagle. A score of three under par on a hole.

drain. Make a long putt.

draw. A controlled moderate curve of the ball from right to left for a right-handed golfer (left to right for a left-handed golfer).

drive. To hit the ball from the tee, usually with a driver.

driver. A one-wood, normally used for the tee shot on par-fours and par-fives.

driving range. An area of a course or free-standing facility for practicing.

drop. To drop a ball from shoulder height on the course, as in the case of an unplayable lie or when the original ball is lost.

duck hook. A low shot that curves hard to the left and downward and usually ends up in an undesirable place.

duffer. An unskilled golfer, also known as a HACKER.

eagle. A score of two under par on a hole.

executive course. A shorter-than-regulation course with a par between 54 and the high 60s.

fade. A controlled moderate curve of the ball from left to right by a right-handed golfer (right to left for a left-handed golfer).

fairway. The closely mown grass that is the main avenue of play from the tee to the green.

fairway wood. Any club having the shape or characteristics of a wooden club, normally used for hitting off the fairway. Could be made out of metal or wood.

fat. A poor golf shot resulting from hitting the ground before the ball.

featheries. The first golf balls, made from strips of leather stuffed with wet feathers.

flagstick. A stick, or pin, with a flag for showing the position of the hole on a green.

flex. The flexibility, or stiffness, of the shaft of a golf club.

flyer. A shot that flies higher and farther than you want it to.

fore. The warning yelled when an errant shot is hit toward someone.

foursome. A group of four golfers playing a round of golf.

fried egg. A ball half-buried in the sand; a very difficult golf shot.

fringe. See collar.

frog hair. The short grass around a green, normally called the apron or collar.

front nine. The first nine holes of an eighteen-hole course.

GCSAA. Golf Course Superintendents Association of America.

GHIN. Golf Handicap Information Network. The nationwide system, developed by the USGA, to calculate handicaps.

gimme. A short putt so close to the hole that your playing partners give it to you without your having to putt the ball. A practice not within the rules but customary in casual golf.

gorse. Area of a golf course thick with shrubs and grass from where it's difficult to play.

grain. The direction in which the blades of grass on a green predominantly point or lie.

green. The area of a hole designed for putting. The best-manicured area of the course.

green fee. A fee charged a golfer for use of a golf course.

greenkeeper. The man or woman responsible for golf course maintenance, more commonly known as the superintendent.

grip. The part of the club held by the golfer, normally made from rubber or leather.

grooves. The indented lines on the clubface used to impart spin on the ball.

gross score. The score before the deduction of your handicap.

grounded. When the sole of a golf club touches the ground.

ground under repair. An area of the course undergoing maintenance from which a golfer may remove his ball without penalty.

gutta ball. Circa 1850 golf ball made out of pitch from the gutta-percha tree.

hacker. An unskilled player, or duffer.

halve. In match play, to tie on a hole with your competitor.

handicap. An allowance in strokes given to a golfer to compensate for different abilities, allowing golfers to compete together on an equitable basis.

hazard. Any obstructive or difficult feature of a golf course such as ponds, lakes, sand traps, or bunkers.

head cover. Protective cover, usually for woods.

heel. The part of the clubhead closest to the shaft or hosel.

hole in one. A score of one on a hole.

honor. The privilege of teeing off first on a hole, decided by a coin toss or the low score from the previous hole.

hook. A shot that curves strongly from right to left and which normally ends up left of a right-handed player's target (directions are opposite for a left-handed golfer).

hosel. The hollow portion of the clubhead where the shaft is attached, sometimes called the neck, or the shank.

in the leather. A gimme putt no farther from the hole than the grip or leather wrapping on a putter.

initiation fee. The up-front fee paid to join a private club.

iron. Type of club with a thin metal clubhead, usually numbered one through nine in addition to a pitching wedge and a sand wedge.

jail, in. When a ball is in a position that requires a very difficult shot.

keeper of the greens. Original name for the course superintendent.

kolven. Dutch game played on ice, often thought to be the predecessor of golf.

lag. To purposely play a long putt close to and short of the hole, not wanting to risk hitting the ball far past the hole.

layout. The design of the golf course.

lie. The position of a ball on the course. Also, the angle at which the clubhead is set on the shaft.

line. The intended path of play.

links. The golf course. Used properly, it refers to a golf course situated on a seaside terrain.

lip. The rim of the hole. A putt that lips out, or goes around the rim of the hole without falling in.

loft. The degree to which the clubface is laid back from vertical, designed to lift the ball into the air.

long irons. The low-lofted lengthier irons used for hitting the ball longer distances.

loose impediments. Unattached and inanimate objects such as twigs, stones, and trash. These may be removed without penalty, except in a hazard.

LPGA. Ladies Professional Golf Association.

major championships. Professional tournaments considered the most important within the golf community. The four recognized major championships for men are the Masters, the U.S. Open, the British Open, and the PGA Championship. For women, the four majors are the Dinah Shore Classic, the LPGA Championship, the du Maurier Classic, and the U.S. Women's Open.

marker. A small object, such as a coin, used to mark the position of the ball that has been lifted on a green.

match play. A competition by holes between two sides where one side defeats the other by having won more holes than there are holes left to play.

medal play. A competition where the winner is determined by the player with the lowest score in strokes.

mulligan. A second-chance shot, usually off the first tee. Common only in friendly matches, illegal according to the rules.

nassau. A common bet in golf consisting of a bet on the front nine, back nine, and entire eighteen.

net score. A golfer's score after the deduction of a handicap.

nickel. Slang term for a five-iron.

nineteenth hole. The bar and grill at a golf club or course.

one putt. To hole the ball on your first putt.

out of bounds. The ground on which play is prohibited, indicated by white stakes or a white line on the ground. When out of bounds, the player must return to the spot from which the shot was played and play another ball, adding one penalty stroke.

outside agency. Any object, including a person, that stops, deflects, or moves a ball in play.

par. The standard score in strokes assigned to a hole based on how an excellent player would score on the hole.

penalty stroke. A stroke added to your score for a violation of the rules.

perimeter weighted. A clubhead design where the majority of weight is distributed around the club's perimeter. Generally considered easier to hit and good for beginners.

PGA. The Professional Golfers' Association of America, the ruling body of American professional golf.

PGA Tour. Professional Golfers' Association Tour. Organization for touring professional golfers that administers more than forty tournaments a year at sites throughout the United States. The "major leagues" of golf.

pin. Slang term for the flagstick.

pitch. An approach shot to the green—less than a full swing but longer than a chip.

play through. To pass a group of slower golfers playing ahead of your group.

playing lesson. A lesson given on the golf course that deals with course management and strategy.

posture. One of the preshot basics of body positioning taught in a golf lesson.

pot bunker. A deep sand trap with very steep sides.

private course. A course that is open only to members and their guests.

provisional ball. A ball played after a previous shot is believed to be out of bounds or lost.

public course. A golf course where the public may play by paying a green fee.

punch. A low, controlled shot played with a shorter swing.

putt. A stroke made on the green with a putter.

putter. A club designed for putting, generally with little loft and shorter in length than all the other clubs in your bag.

quail high. A shot hit on a low, flat trajectory.

recovery. A shot played back into a satisfactory position from the rough, hazard, or any other undesirable place.

relief. Permission given under the rules to lift and drop the ball without penalty.

resort course. Course located in a vacation or destination area such as Las Vegas, Hilton Head, the Bahamas, or Palm Springs.

rough. The playable grounds of a golf course where the grass is longer and heavier than the fairway.

Royal and Ancient. One of the two governing

bodies in golf that establish the rules of the game. Headquartered in St. Andrews, Scotland.

rub of the green. Any accident, not caused by a golfer or his caddy, that moves or stops the ball. Whether the result goes for or against the golfer depends on an element of luck.

sand trap. A pit or depression filled with sand. Also referred to as a bunker.

sand wedge. A specially designed club for use in a sand trap but also used to hit out of grass.

sandbagger. A golfer who turns in only his or her higher scores to artificially inflate his or her handicap, thus making it easier to score well in handicapped competition. A cheater.

scratch golfer. An excellent player whose handicap is zero.

scramble. A tournament format, most common in corporate and charity golf outings, that allows players of all abilities to contribute to a team score.

semiprivate course. Course with members that allows limited outside play.

shaft. The long, thin part of the club, enclosed by a grip at the top and attached to a clubhead at the bottom.

shank. The most dreaded shot in golf, hit off the hosel of the club and straight to the right.

sidespin. The spin imparted on a golf ball when struck causing it to curve left or right.

skull. To hit a poor shot with the leading edge of the club, causing the ball to run or fly low and end up well beyond the target.

sky. To hit a shot that unintentionally travels extremely high and short.

slice. A shot that curves strongly from left to right and ends up right of the intended target for a right-handed golfer (directions are opposite for a left-handed golfer). The most common ball flight for the beginning golfer.

slope index. Complex mathematical calculation used to measure the relative difficulty of a particular course. Used in developing handicaps.

snake. An extremely long putt that winds back and forth over several undulations in the green.

sole. The bottom of the clubhead (noun). Also, to ground the club at address (verb).

stableford. A common tournament format in which players earn points on each hole depending on their score.

staking it. Slang expression for hitting a shot close to the flagstick.

stance. The positioning of a player's feet at address. One of the basic fundamentals of golf.

stiff. To hit a ball very close to the hole. Also, a certain flex in a golf shaft.

stroke. A player's action in striking the ball, added to the player's score.

sudden death. A form of playoff in which tied players play extra holes to determine a winner. The winner is the first player to score lower than the other on a particular hole.

summer rules. A term for playing the ball as it lies, as the rules state you should.

superintendent. The official in charge of maintaining the golf course. Also known as the greenkeeper.

surlyn. A man-made type of plastic material from which the covers of golf balls are made. Ideal for the beginning golfer because it resists cutting.

sweet spot. The ideal spot on the clubface to hit the ball, resulting in a shot with a particularly good feeling.

swing thoughts. Ideas a player keeps on his or her mind during a swing.

takeaway. The start of the golf swing.

tap in. To hole a very short putt.

tee. A peg on which the ball is placed. Also, the point from which play of a hole begins, the teeing ground.

tee off. To play a tee shot.

tee shot. A shot played from a tee or teeing ground. Your first shot on a hole.

tee time. The prearranged reservation time for beginning a round of golf.

Texas wedge. A shot played with a putter from off the green.

thin. A shot where the ball strikes the sole of the club, resulting in a very poor shot.

three putt. To take three putts to hole the ball on a green. These are to be avoided.

threesome. Three golfers playing in a group.

toe. The part of the clubhead farthest from the shaft or hosel.

top. To hit the ball above its center. A shot that usually dives downward, rolls on the ground, and travels a short distance.

turn. The halfway point in an eighteen-hole round after nine holes have been played.

twosome. Two golfers playing together.

unplayable lie. A ball too difficult to play as it lies such that the player must proceed by moving the ball under penalty of one stroke.

up and down. Hitting out of a bunker or other trouble, and into the hole in two shots, including one putt.

USGA. United States Golf Association, one of the ruling bodies of golf.

wedge. An iron club used for short shots, sometimes called a pitching wedge or ten-iron.

whiff. A swing and a miss, counted as a stroke.

winter rules. Allowing golfers to improve their lie within six inches of where the ball originally lay without penalty. Often used during the winter, or after poor weather, so as to not make the playing conditions too difficult.

wood. Any club having a wooden head or having the head and general design characteristics of a wooden-headed club. Could be made out of metal.

wrapped up in the flag. When the descending ball from a shot right on target gets caught in the flag before dropping right next to, or even in, the hole.

yips. A chronic missing of short putts due to nervousness or twitching of the hands.